THIS BOOK
IS LOVINGLY DEDICATED
TO THE MEMORY OF
NANA, DADDY,
MY UNCLE TOM
AND CLARA JANE STARR

CUCINA PRESS, LTD.
OLALLA, WASHINGTON
1992

ISBN 0-9635334-0-1

Cover Design and Artwork by Laurel Black

Back Cover Photo by Victoria Artist Tess Morgan

FORWARD

Hi!

I'm Victoria of Victoria's Bella Cucina. VBC is a company which makes and sells a variety of fresh pesto sauces for pasta. Our sauces range from the traditional basil to garlic artichoke, and are marketed as *PESTO PESTO*. I grew up in the grocery and specialty food business, but worked in human services for years. When I "burned out", friends urged me to try to support myself and Finnegan (the Cat) doing something I loved: cooking. Michel Lalanne and Daisy Langley beat me senseless with that strategy one lazy summer in Ketchum, Idaho. Risky, but it made sense.

Back home that fall, I experimented with the family pesto recipe. Most people think that pesto means Basil---pesto just means ground or pounded. You can literally grind or pound anything, and I did. Gradually a group of new flavors emerged.

Chiquita and Tom test-marketed them in A Seafood Market in Lower Hadlock---just across from the Ajax Cafe, Port Townsend, Washington's answer to Cannery Row. Dick McMillian of Backyard Gourmet Barbecue Sauce was my "coach." Laurel Black had the faith in me to design a label and brochure on "spec". BA, Linda and The Bear gave tremendous moral support. Teresa staunchly tried the first batch of

Sun-dried Tomato pesto, saying "maybe it looks better in the light."

The products were well-received by the public. Then, local restaurants and markets bought it. Today when I'm in the stores demonstrating *PESTO PESTO* fresh pasta sauces, people say, "this stuff is great, but how do I use it?" It's time to tell.

Author Nora Ephron said pesto was the "quiche of the eighties"---I say it is the gourmet staple of the nineties. You can put it on anything except chocolate and ice cream and I'm working on that. Pesto is the way to season freshly without an herb garden---perfect for the gourmet on the go who still wishes to eat well.

This book includes recipes for the casual, the calculated and the emergency gourmet. Most are for the first two categories, for that is the beauty of pesto. Those who cook for fun or therapy will love the recipe where a turkey begs to be boned. There are also recipes for those of you who just want something different on your toast and eggs in the morning.

I hope this will tell you everything you wanted to know about pesto but weren't certain who to ask. There is relatively little mystery to pesto ---it is quick and elegant. It is easier to prepare a gourmet meal with pesto than change lanes on

I-5 under the Convention Center. So, like the song says, "have a good time".

Victoria

ACKNOWLEDGEMENTS

There are many people without whose support this book would not have been completed. Heartfelt thanks to Laurel Black, Mr. Safety and Kim for their encouragement, design and editing support. Thanks to Finnegan the Cat for sitting by the computer during periods of author frustration. Thanks to Tess Morgan, Victoria artist, who captured my soul in the cover photo.

Notes:

iv FORWARD

Notes:

TABLE OF CONTENTS

vi

Notes:

About Pesto

Victoria's Bella Cucina

Victoria's Bella Cucina makes many pesto sauces. Throughout this book you will see that I like a variety of pestos. However, it is important to note that while I like to use all the flavors, basil pesto is still a good all-around pasta sauce and seasoning. Those of you who have a freezer full of basil pesto, please understand my bias and do not be limited or intimidated by it.

Please approach this book with a spirit of adventure and an eye to experimenting with your own recipes, beyond the ones contained herein. I would like you to get acquainted with pesto the spice. Use it for pasta---it's wonderful, but start thinking about how you can kill several birds with one stone by using pesto. It allows you to use fresh or frozen seasoning without finding and keeping an arsenal of fresh herbs in your vegetable keeper. Not everyone has their own herb garden or lives down the hill from Cedarbrook Herb Farm.

Here is my basic basil pesto recipe---I'm afraid the others are a trade secret for now. The other flavors besides Basil can be found at local markets, or you may special order them from us using the mail order form in this book.

BASIC PESTO RECIPE

5 cups basil leaves
1 cup fresh parsley (I like Italian flat leaf
    parsley)
3/4 cup olive oil
3 large cloves of garlic---but I use 5 (yes, 5 big
    ones)
1/2 cup parmesan, or romano cheese
1/2 teaspoon fresh marjoram
1/2 cup walnuts, almonds or pine nuts
2 tablespoons bottled lemon juice (5 percent
    acidity)

Yields about 2 cups of pesto

Rinse basil and parsley well in cold water and
remove the tough central stems. Place the leaves
in the food processor or blender. Add oil, garlic,
marjoram, walnuts, lemon juice and cheese and
blend until thoroughly homogenized.

Those of you who make your own pesto will
question the use of lemon juice, but given the
level of concern these days regarding the
potential for botulism with garlic, this is a must.
The lemon juice acidifies the mixture to prevent
the growth of harmful bacteria. We've all been
making pesto for years without this precaution,
but just look at it as new technology which will
improve your sauce.

Pesto must always be refrigerated, preferably with a thin layer of olive oil on top. As long as you use the lemon juice to increase the acidity you should be able to keep it in your refrigerator for awhile; however, pesto freezes beautifully and I suggest freezing in a shallow container and then cutting it into several portions for storage in a ziplock bag. Pesto should keep in the freezer for a year. Some folks recommend freezing it in ice cube trays, but I have plastic trays and they never lose the hint of garlic after being used to freeze pesto. Garlic does not lend a gracious overtone to lemonade or gin.

Some people only want to make pesto with extra virgin olive oil---they like that strong olive oil taste. I use a lighter olive oil because I want to taste the herbs. When test- marketing *PESTO PESTO*, the most important feedback we received from buyers and chefs was that they liked the fact that they could taste the herbs and not the heaviness of the olive oil. Many other customers say they like *PESTO PESTO* because it isn't "oily."

The recipes in this book, with a few exceptions, do not fall into the category of being "classic" anything. In my mind touting a recipe as resulting in a "classic" dish means absolutely nothing if the end result doesn't suit your individual tastes. Consider if you will: Haggis.

4 ABOUT PESTO

My pestos are not classic. They are not all basil flavored. They have less oil, less salt and less cheese, but people tell me that they really like the taste, and in the end analysis it really does get reduced to a *love affair with taste.*

This book should an idea-starter, not an oracle. While I wrote it I imagined that I'm talking to you on the telephone or we're sitting in the kitchen trading ideas. We're swapping recipes. In fact, if you have recipes you want to share please send them to me, and I will pass them on.

Finally, I think it was Ernest Hemingway who said, "the right thing is what feels good afterwards". This has a great deal of import for the area of food, particularly in this age of complex recipes and cooking "bibles". The best advice ever given to me came from the Executive Chef at the old Francisco's in Seattle. He introduced me to the use of fennel and taught me to stop being creatively constipated by cookbooks and specific recipes. He told me to use the books for ideas, and then strike out on my own and experiment. And so I say to you: Do what feels right and tastes good---if you make a mistake, learn from it. If it's really bad, feed it to the dog or dump it and do it differently the next time---but by all means ---go for it!

APPETIZERS & FUN FOOD

Victoria's Bella Cucina

BOFFO BREADS

Mix pesto to taste with softened butter---I recommend half butter and half pesto for the greens and 1/3 pesto to 2/3 butter with the Sun-dried Tomato.

Brush pure pesto or pesto butter on halved loaves of french or italian bread and sprinkle with parmesan or mozzarella. Run under a pre-heated broiler until cheese is bubbly and slightly browned. Serve as an appetizer or with dinner.

Brush pure pesto or pesto butter on focaccia. This can be done before or after heating---I like to slice the bread and layer it with pesto and cheese. This works very well with the garlic focaccia from the Fairfield bakery. This loaf is fairly tall and easy to work with in terms of layering.

Spread Boboli bread shells with pesto, artichoke hearts and cheese---place in a pre-heated broiler until cheese melts and bubbles, slice and serve. Add more toppings to a larger crust and serve with a salad for a meal.

Serve mini-bagels, cream cheese and pesto as an appetizer.

Make pesto rounds by slicing baguettes thinly and brushing with pesto butter. Bake at 350°

for 3 to 4 minutes, cool and serve with cheese. I recommend brie, chevre or boursin.

PESTO VOLCANO

1 loaf crusty italian or french bread
1/2 pound to 1 pound brie---peppered or plain
1/2 cup pesto mixed with 2 tablespoons olive oil

Go to an italian or french bakery and buy a round loaf of peasant bread or a nice crusty loaf of french bread.

Hollow out the bread and cut or tear excised bread into chunks. (I like to tear it because it's asymmetrical, more interesting and my mother would hate it.) Fill the hollow with regular or pepper brie cut into chunks. Most people remove the rind but I like to see what various people do with it so I leave it on as a form of social research. Sometimes I put a layer of pesto on the cheese midway through the filling of the bread cavity. Slice into the crust so that people can pull it off the loaf when it comes out of the oven. Place in a 400° oven---or if you're good with bread in the microwave you can use that. Leave the bread in until the brie bubbles, then drizzle any pesto on top of the cheese and serve with bread chunks.

CHEESES CHEESES

In an emergency you can simply pour pesto over brie or cream cheese that has spent thirty seconds in the microwave---serve with melba, Tuscany toast or crackers/chips of choice. This is also great with the pesto rounds found in this section. Or in a real emergency*---plain french bread. Faced with brie, pesto or cream cheese, your friends and relatives will find a way to make it work for them.

PESTO CHEESE SPREAD

Mix 1/2 to 1 cup pesto with 1 cup of cream cheese, Quark (low fat substitute available in most large supermarkets), ricotta or blended cottage cheese and serve on crackers or tuscany toast or french bread. You can also mix the same amount of pesto with shredded mozzarella, jack or cheddar. Spread mixture on crackers or toast rounds and place under pre-heated broiler until cheese melts and bubbles.

*This book concludes with a must-have list for the emergency gourmet. Look for it---it may someday save your social life.

SALMON PATE

1 tall can of good salmon, boned, or 1-1/2 cups
    fresh cooked salmon
8 ounces cream cheese
1/2 cup pecans or walnuts, chopped
1/2 cup pesto; cooks' choice

Blend all ingredients except nuts in the bowl of
the food processor. When well blended, remove
and shape into a ball or log and roll in chopped
nuts. Serve with crackers, bagel chips, french
bread or toast rounds.

VICTORIA'S HOLIDAY PESTO TORTE

This is a favorite with everyone. It is an
excruciatingly simple recipe that will be warmly
received by guests.

1 pound cream cheese
1/2 cup green pesto (Basil or Peppercorn)
1/2 cup red pesto (Sun-dried Tomato)
1/2 cup chopped walnuts or pine nuts

Soften cream cheese. This may be done by
adding a bit of sour cream, warm water or
softened butter and beating with a power mixer.
The emergency gourmet adds a bit of warm
water and throws the cream cheese in the
microwave. Line a loaf pan or molded pan with

plastic wrap or waxed paper. Layer one third of the cream cheese in the bottom of the pan and add a layer of the red pesto---use it all. Sprinkle 1/4 cup of nuts on the pesto. Add a second layer of cream cheese and then use the green pesto and the remainder of the nuts. Top with the remaining 1/3 of the cream cheese. Press into pan and refrigerate for several hours. Emergency gourmets can throw it in the freezer for 45 minutes.

When firm turn onto serving dish, be sure to remove the plastic wrap, and serve with french bread, crackers or toast rounds. This is a really tasty treat that you can make quickly in your kitchen---before demos I always wait until the last minute, then decide to make a torte at midnight for the following day. It takes me about twenty minutes to do five pounds. It would probably take less time in the daylight and if made by some who had good motor skills. You will find it very costly in the deli cheese section, and a little short on pesto. So go for it. Make it at home.

This torte can also be layered in a mold, but I like the way it looks sliced.

BRIE TORTE

Slice a cold firm wedge of brie laterally into three even layers, keeping rind intact. Layer with your favorite pesto or pestos.

Serve at room temperature with crackers or french bread. The emergency or casual gourmets can run it into the microwave for a bit if so desired. If the brie is really ripe, stick it in the freezer for a few minutes to firm it up, and use a knife warmed in water to cut each slice.

DIPS

Pesto really is the penultimate weapon in the war against boring dips. All it takes is a 1/2 cup of any pesto with a cup of sour cream or Quark and you are ready to go. The flavor is so well-married in the body of the pesto that it arrives immediately---no waiting and tasting to see if the de-hydrated vegetables from the soup mix are ready yet. Pesto dips go from bowl and spoon to eager guests. Add a little mayonnaise if you like.

Of course, my favorite is the Green Peppercorn, but I also like the Basil and Garlic Artichoke.

Serve with crudities, crackers or chips. Use remainder as a condiment for fish or meat. It can also be tossed with cold pasta and steamed vegetables for a pasta salad.

ARTICHOKE DIP GOES PESTO

Finnegan the cat and I love artichokes. When I test-demonstrated the Artichoke *PESTO PESTO*, someone shared her favorite artichoke dip with me and I have modified it with pesto. It is a great dip.

1 cup parmesan or mozzarella cheese
1 can artichokes, drained and unmarinated
fresh garlic to taste
1 small can diced chilies or,
1 cup pesto (Basil, Peppercorn, Artichoke)

Mix all ingredients together in an ovenproof dish then bake at 350° for 30 minutes. Remove from oven and serve immediately with crackers, chips or breads.

Remember that you may substitute Quark for sour cream and cream cheese in many of these recipes. I haven't used it, but my low-fat conscious friends swear by it. You can also use low-fat yogurt.

RED PESTO DIPS

The red pesto, Sun-dried Tomato, is a real pleasure. People eat it straight from the container on a variety of crackers chips and breads. It makes a great sauce for pizza, or add a little to a bottled spaghetti sauce. When I demonstrate the pestos in stores, the men and children, culturally leery of anything green, want to taste the red pesto first. They always love it. I hope you will too.

Mix Sun-dried tomato pesto with 2 to 4 tablespoons of olive oil and serve as a dip or condiment.

Mix 1/2 cup red pesto with sour cream or Quark and serve with chips.

Thin red pesto with 2 to 4 tablespoons of olive oil and pour over a block of cream cheese. Top with crabmeat, shrimp or imitation seafood and a dollop of sour cream. Serve with crackers or toast rounds.

DOLLOP: This is a very arcane subjective measurement. It is used to denote any amount from a tablespoon to an ice cream scoop and allows the cook to exercise their judgment and preference. Dollop is also an invertogram.

SEAFOOD SAUCE OR DIP

Mix 1/2 cup Basil, Peppercorn or Garlic Artichoke pesto with 1 cup of sour cream and 2 tablespoons of mayonnaise. Serve as a condiment. Can be served immediately or chilled until meal time.

NACHOS PESTO

The flavor of pesto goes well with the flavor of corn and thus can be used to put a new twist in an old treat.

RED NACHOS

Sun-dried Tomato pesto with 2 tablespoons of olive oil. Use the pesto in place of salsa. Layer chips with sauce and cheeses, finishing with cheese. Place in 400° oven until cheese bubbles and browns slightly. You can also use the microwave if desired. Optional: Drizzle more pesto on top when serving.

GREEN NACHOS

Thin one of the green pesto sauces with 2 tablespoons of olive oil and use in place of salsa. Layer chips with sauce and cheeses, finishing with cheese. Place in a 400° oven until cheese

is bubbly and slightly browned. Optional:
Drizzle more pesto on top when serving.

Saving the best for last----------

SCALLOPS IN PESTO

This is my favorite appetizer and frequent
evening meal.

1/4 pound scallops per person (tiny bay
    scallops are best)
1/2 to 1 pound fresh sliced mushrooms
1 tablespoon olive oil and 1 teaspoon butter
8 ounces (one container) Green Peppercorn,
    Basil, or Artichoke Pesto
1 tablespoon wine per person
lime wedges, or lemons if you prefer
Crusty french or italian bread

Put the bread in oven to heat.

Saute mushrooms lightly (2 minutes) in oil and
butter. Rinse scallops under cold running water
and drain on paper towels. Combine scallops
and mushrooms in a shallow oval dish and add
pesto mixed with wine. You can do this in
individual ramekins if desired. Cover with
plastic wrap and perforate wrap with a knife in
several spots. Cook in microwave on high for 1
minute.

Garnish with squeezes of lime and serve with wedges of heated french bread and cocktail forks.

This dish can also be prepared in a non-stick pan and then transferred to one large or individual serving dishes. To prepare in this manner add scallops to sauted mushrooms. Saute scallops for one minute then add pesto and wine, heat through and serve. It makes a great meal when coupled with a green salad.

SHRIMP PESTO

3 to 4 medium or large shrimp per person (or
    6---consider the company and the appetite)
1/2 to 1 pound sliced fresh mushrooms
2 tablespoons olive oil and 1 teaspoon butter
8 ounces Peppercorn, Basil or Garlic Artichoke
    pesto
1 tablespoon wine per person
lemon wedges
crusty french or italian bread heated in oven

Prepare as above, but if sauteing the shrimp start them with the mushrooms and cook until light pink. Then add the pesto mixed with wine and heat through. For the microwave, saute the mushrooms just until heated through, add shrimp and pesto mixed with wine, cover and microwave for 2 minutes on high. Serve with french bread and a squeeze of lemon.

Try the shrimp with Sun-dried Tomato and red wine instead of white and green.

Again, this makes a great meal in minutes!! Serve with green salad. For an entree serve over cooked pasta in shallow bowls.

Notes:

BREAKFAST

Victoria's Bella Cucina

Some people find the taste of garlic and herbs in the morning impossible. The people I know seem to find the thought of morning impossible without the infusion of garlic and herbs. This chapter is dedicated to the latter.

SHARKEY'S FRIED EGGS

Sharkey tends bar at the Valley Tavern in Chimacum, Washington, but he used to be at A Seafood Place in Lower Hadlock, where he became addicted to the flavor of pesto.

1 to 2 eggs per person (preferably from chickens who do aerobics*)
1 tablespoon olive oil
1 teaspoon Pesto per egg
    Suggested pesto flavors: Basil, Green Peppercorn, Sun-dried Tomato, Garlic Artichoke

* It is my understanding that chickens who are allowed to get out and roam around and clutter up the yard produce eggs which are lower in cholesterol than their nest-sitting, commercial egg ranch counterparts. If you have the opportunity, know something about the school the chickens who produce your eggs attend.

Place olive oil and a teaspoon of pesto in a non-stick fry pan and cook eggs, basting with oil and pesto. When done to personal perfection remove to platter and drizzle with remaining pesto. Serve additional pesto on the side for eager eaters and those who like to travel around their plates with toast.

SCRAMBLED EGGS VICTORIA

Lightly scramble four eggs with 1/2 cup cubed cream cheese. When done, place eggs on serving platter and top with your favorite pesto. I like the Green Peppercorn, Garlic Artichoke and Sun-dried Tomato. Serve with herbed biscuits or corn bread---toast, if you're like me and in a hurry. This dish goes well served with pork sausage and melon.

For four eggs, use 1/2 cup of pesto and then serve the rest on the side to accommodate individual tastes.

FRITTATA PESTO

Mix 1/4 to 1/2 cup pesto sauce with your favorite frittata and then drizzle a bit more on top for garnish before serving.

For a frittata, lightly saute sliced vegetables and meat or seafood, in a non-stick pan. Add eggs calculated to address the hunger of your horde, beat the eggs lightly with pesto and add to pan. When bottom is set add 1/2 to 1 cup of a favorite cheese and run the frittata under a pre-heated broiler until cheese bubbles and browns slightly. Drizzle pesto mixed with a little olive oil on top and serve.

PESTO QUICHE

Add 1/4 to 1/2 cup of any pesto sauce to your favorite quiche when mixing, and then drizzle pesto on top when it comes out of the oven.

Not recommended for chocolate quiche.

THE PESTO OMELET

2 eggs
1 tablespoon half and half, or milk
1 tablespoon Artichoke, Basil, Garlic Artichoke
   or Green Peppercorn or Cilantro pesto
ground black or seasoned pepper, to taste
olive oil mist, 1 tablespoon olive oil or butter

Lightly beat the eggs, cream, pesto and pepper in a small bowl. Use mist, oil or butter in a non-stick pan over medium heat. Add mixture and when bubbling around the edges gently stir mixture toward center of the pan without breaking through to the bottom. When the bottom is set but the top is still wet, slide omelet onto a plate, but keep one half of the omelet in the pan to fold over the portion on the plate (tricky but you can do it). Sprinkle on parmesan cheese on before folding over, and serve immediately.

This is also good with a little crab or shrimp, or you can crumble in a bit of cooked italian sausage. With the addition of seafood you might serve wedges of lemon or lime, and if you're really fond of yourself and your breakfast mate---ripe avocado. I always use any excuse to throw in artichoke hearts. I'm not personally very fond of eggs, but you can use them to sort of hold together other things that you like. Then there are the pickled or blanched asparagus spears---finish this paragraph with a personal food touch.

Double recipe for each additional person, or for yourself after kayaking to the lighthouse and getting stuck in the oyster strings coming back. This lends new meaning to morning hunger.

EGGS PESTO ALFREDO

I love eggs benedict but I hate to make hollandaise sauce, and the prepared mixes are, in my estimation, icky. Now, I will eat anything if it sports hollandaise, but if I have to make it the enthusiasm wanes. I seem to only get the spirit moving during the holidays. The rest of the time

I do the emergency gourmet and call on Pesto Alfredo. Then with the leftovers I have his brother Pasta Alfredo cater the evening meal.

2 poached eggs per person
1 toasted english muffin or 2 crumpets/person
8 ounces prepared alfredo sauce
4 to 8 ounces pesto depending on taste
sliced canadian bacon or sliced smoked salmon
1/2 to 1 cup grated parmesan or romano

This is a pretty routine dish. I do the sauce first. I always have a use for the leftover sauce because it is great on pasta for dinner. I mix 8 ounces of pesto with 8 ounces of Alfredo sauce and place in a microwaveable pitcher or measuring cup. My personal favorite is the Green Peppercorn, but any of the green pestos are great.

You can also add pesto to a prepared hollandaise or white sauce.

Poach eggs and toast muffins, top with canadian bacon or salmon. Serve in ramekins or on plates topped with sauce heated 2 to 3 minutes in the microwave. Use as much sauce as you want ---I'm not going to limit you to the ritual 2 tablespoons. Use remaining sauce with pasta for the evening meal.

ITALIAN SCRAMBLE

2 links Italian sausage, removed from casings or
    thinly sliced
1 cup sliced mushrooms
1/4 cup sliced onions
1/4 cup sliced red or green pepper
4 to 6 large eggs (preferably aerobic chickens)

Use a non-stick fry pan and 1 tablespoon olive
oil or olive oil mist. Slice sausage and saute
until done. Drain on paper towels and return to
pan with a bit more oil or mist and the
vegetables and a tablespoon of Basil, Peppercorn
or Sun-dried Tomato pesto. Saute vegetables
lightly (2 to 3 minutes) then scramble with eggs.
When eggs are set to your liking remove to
serving platter and serve with pesto drizzled on
top or on the side.

Note: Depending on the consistency of the pesto
you may want to thin it just a bit with olive oil
so that it will "drizzle" more effectively. Try
this dish with chorizo and the red pesto.

NORMAN'S PESTO TOAST

This dish is best with the garlic foccacia from
the Fairfield Bakery in Victoria, but sometimes I
just have to force myself to use another bread.
My emergency frozen food supply does,
however, always contain this bread. The

customs people think I'm nuts because I only buy bread, and come back with a suitcase full.

You were there for twenty-four hours---why did you need a suitcase? For the focaccia, of course, and then there is the sourdough wheat. Need I say more?

Which pesto? We like the Green Peppercorn. Norman Bradley likes the Sun-dried Tomato.

Put pesto to taste on toasted/heated bread, cover with cheese and run under the broiler until slightly brown or bubbly-depending on cheeses used.

Suggested cheeses: Ricotta, low fat cottage cheese, mozzarella, parmesan, jack, or in an emergency---cheddar.

PESTO CORNBREAD

You can cheat and use a good mix if you are in a hurry. I didn't know until I came home from college early one weekend, that my mother used a mix for cornbread--obviously I didn't empty the garbage---an American family tragedy, but not significant enough to stop the gourmet on the run. Most of the mixes on the market are fairly good and the addition of pesto makes discernment less of an issue than time and mess. Just add 1/2 cup pesto to any mix and you have it. Of course, don't forget to add the other ingredients called for in the mix directions.

If determined to make your own, try the following:

1/2 cup flour---sift it if you need to kill time
1-1/2 cups yellow corn meal
1 teaspoon salt
1 tablespoon baking powder
3 eggs, well beaten
1 cup milk
1/4 cup cream
1/4 cup melted butter
1/2 cup any flavor pesto

Mix together all dry ingredients, add the eggs and milk and beat thoroughly. Add cream, pesto and butter and mix completely. Pour into an 8-1/2 x 11 pan sprayed with pam or buttered and bake in a 400° oven for 15 to 18 minutes.

These are great with ham or sausage and if you have any left you can make bite-sized sandwiches---let breakfast guests make it up as they go along. When faced with a new food, particularly one that goes well with butter, people will rise to the challenge.

PESTO BISCUITS

Biscuits spiked with pesto are marvelous breakfast, brunch or soup fare. They are easy to make by adding 2 tablespoons of your favorite pesto to a regular baking powder or buttermilk biscuit. Here's a basic recipe:

2 cups all-purpose flour
1 tablespoon baking powder
1/4 cup butter or shortening
3/4 cup milk or half and half (when in doubt go
    for the cream)
2 tablespoons pesto, any flavor

Sift dry ingredients into a bowl and cut in the shortening or butter. Add the pesto and milk and stir quickly until the dough clings together. Turn out on a floured board and knead a few times, pat or roll out to 1/2 inch thickness and cut into rounds with biscuit cutter or the edge of a drinking glass. A drinking glass dipped in flour is a great biscuit cutter. My grandmother, Clara Jane Starr, always used a drinking glass to cut out biscuits because she could never find the biscuit cutter in her pantry arsenal. When she passed away I found it in the flour bin and still use it.

Place biscuits on a greased cookie sheet or greased biscuit pan and bake at 450° for about 12 to 15 minutes or until lightly browned. Serve immediately.

I would suggest a way to use them on a second meal, but they never make it to the second meal. I sometimes make them especially for picnic or skiing fare, alone or as a sandwich.

One of the great traditions in my family is the Old Pot Shower. Whenever anyone gets married or sets up housekeeping, the rest of the family and close friends throw the Old Pot Shower and each person gives the bride one of her favorite used and broken-in cooking utensils. These articles are the most reliable, oft-used and treasured cookware in my kitchen.

Notes:

SANDWICHES

Victoria's Bella Cucina

Again, we have to get into image-busting. Pesto isn't just basil and it isn't just for pasta. It is a wonderful seasoning for all sorts of soups and is a tasty addition to many sandwiches. Our favorites in this category are Green Peppercorn or Garlic Artichoke with white meats, cold pork and lamb and seafoods and the Sun-dried Tomato with fowl and meatloaf. Use pesto as you would any other condiment, such as mustard and mayonnaise. It is dynamite coupled with grilled sandwiches containing cheese.

We won't natter on about sandwiches---use your imagination, but here are a few favorites. The cheese and onion comes with a disclaimer---John's British. We were lucky we got him to try pesto at all.

ROAST BEEF

Those of us who still eat red meat will use Basil or Green Peppercorn Pesto to adorn this old time favorite. I saw some graffiti on the ferry telling us that beef kills---well, frankly, sometimes I would simply kill for beef.

MEATLOAF SANDWICHES
---HOT OR COLD

Traditionally, dijon mustard was my drug of choice with meatloaf sandwiches---now I like to

add pesto. My two favorites are the Green
Peppercorn and the Sun-dried Tomato.

COLD

Use garlic focaccia from Victoria, B.C.'s
Fairfield Bakery (large round loaves about three
or four inches tall and loaded with chunks of
garlic), or console yourself with a good local
sourdough. Lightly butter one slice of bread and
add mayonnaise to taste or conscience. Add
sliced meatloaf and then cover the remaining
slice with pesto. Add lettuce, or other mulch,
and serve with kosher dills. If you are feeling
reckless add some swiss or muenster cheese.

HOT

Lightly butter a slice of good bread and add
mayonnaise to taste---or not. Place sliced
meatloaf cold or hot on bread and top with a
smear of pesto and swiss, muenster or
mozzarella cheese. Run under a pre-heated
broiler until cheese is bubbly and slightly
browned. Add second slice of bread and lettuce,
etc., if desired.

Mustard was also my drug of choice with cold
lamb or pork sandwiches (and corndogs---one at
the fair every year), but again pesto has added a
new dimension. Use as you would a condiment

in the manner outlined for meatloaf. Use Green
Peppercorn, Garlic Artichoke.

Some will put the Sun-dried Tomato on
anything, but this isn't the place for it in my
estimation---up to you though---I didn't drink
coffee for thirty years, now I live for that daily
latte. The Peppercorn is also great on salmon
sandwiches, and on:

JOHN ENTWHISLE'S CHEESE, ONION AND PESTO SANDWICH

I don't know what John Entwhisle usually eats,
but I do know that he was converted to pesto
through a grilled cheese and onion sandwich
with Green Peppercorn pesto. He reportedly
exclaimed, "this can't be this tasty and good for
me, can it?" To which Ronni replied, "Well,
John, it's all natural".

So basically, do a cold or grilled cheese
sandwich with onion and add pesto as you might
add mustard. Again---exercise good judgment
with this one, and don't eat before a promising
evening with a close friend.

SMOKED SALMON WITH CHEESE AND PESTO

Use bread or bagels for this treat---make hero size and serve for lunch or an appetizer.

Add Dill, Garlic Artichoke, Basil or Peppercorn pesto to this old stand-by. Put the pesto on the cream cheese side of the bread or you can mix eight ounces of cream cheese with 1/2 cup of pesto and put on the sandwich in one layer. Use the remainder on muffins in the morning or hot pasta at dinner.

CHICKEN OR TURKEY SANDWICH PESTO, OPEN-FACED

Spread butter, mayonnaise and green or red pesto on a single, but reasonably large slice of bread (cracked wheat sourdough is a winner). Add thinly sliced turkey or chicken and top with swiss cheese. Run under a pre-heated broiler until the cheese is bubbly and slightly browned. I like to add avocado slices below the chicken and next to the pesto. Some may also wish to add a slice of red, Walla Walla Sweet or Maui onion.

CHICKEN OR TURKEY SANDWICH WITH BREAD TIMES TWO

Use the same ingredients as above, but add lettuce if desired. Top with an additional slice of bread and serve cold. Again, I hesitate to specify the number of ounces per sandwich. Years of observation have keenly noted that sandwich ingredients, quantity and preparation are a highly personal and individual matter.

THE MIX AND MATCH PARTY SANDWICH

I never was quite able to put one of those huge sandwiches together and make it stay together-things kept falling out. However, I have friends with better motor skills who can make a huge party sandwich as well as decorate cakes and make their pie crust look like an advertisement in Gourmet.

Those highly skilled individuals tell me that pesto is a great addition to a party sandwich and the one of choice seems to couple the Peppercorn with two or three types of ham, turkey and cheese. I think the Sun-dried Tomato or Basil would also be good with this combination. The Artichoke goes with everything.

PESTO PITA SANDWICH

I like to fill pita bread with chicken or turkey
cubed and mixed with 2 tablespoons of
mayonnaise and 1 to 2 tablespoons of any green
pesto. But Garlic Artichoke is my favorite.
People are funny about their turkey/chicken salad
and their tuna fish. I like to add thin slices of
celery, water chestnuts and slivered almonds. I
also use celery seed and finely minced scallions.
It really depends on what is in the fridge and my
time table. You might want to add chopped
eggs---olives, whatever. Consider this
impressionistic art---whatever it looks like to
you. This is a good times/seat of the pants
recipe for this cookbook--- *Experiment.*

BURGERS

Beef

You can use pesto with burgers as a way to add
variety to an all-time favorite. You may either
mix pesto with the ground beef and broil or use
it as a condiment. One of my favorite
combinations is to add mushrooms sauted in
pesto to a burger, or a combo of mushrooms and
sauted onions. I like to serve them open-faced
because I am a clumsy burger eater. I put so
many things on it that I can't get it cut properly,
or keep everything tidy in the bun. I'm safer
with a plate and cutlery. Sun-dried Tomato is
wonderful with this dish, as is Garlic Artichoke.

Chicken

I really like the pestos with chicken and fish sandwiches and the new ground chicken. Sometimes I do "burgers" with chicken or white fish and add pesto to the combination in lieu of mustard. You can also marinate chicken and fish in pesto before cooking or use as a baste during the cooking process. Use either the greens or the red, or the Garlic Artichoke.

All of the above go well with the cheeses and veggies one might add to a burger.

Notes:

34 SANDWICHES

Notes:

SOUPS

Victoria's Bella Cucina

Pesto can be an exciting addition to soups and seafood stews. Use it as a seasoning--a rule of thumb is to begin with 1 tablespoon per quart of soup stock, then adjust to your personal taste.

A few quick ideas: Add to packaged chicken or turkey soups to create some distinction from the cafeteria, and definitely add to homemade chicken and turkey soups (all the greens), cheese soups (greens), minestrone (reds), beef barley (Peppercorn). Put a light touch---a couple of tablespoons---in seafood chowder or stew and use liberally for the best cioppino in town.

Cioppino is one of those very expensive restaurant dishes that has a certain mystique (order 24 hours in advance). The origins are very humble and the only mystery of its history is the rigid definition of its contents, specifically the seafood. Italian and mediterranean fishermen made it on a bonfire at the beach and sometimes it cooked for two or three days with an addition of something every now and then. Therein lies the mystery---what didn't get sold went into the pot. I do it in a crock pot and it usually cooks twice---the original and the reheat. I really like it better the second day. Face it---seafood is always tasty, so the key is the sauce. The key to the cioppino sauce that Harry Watkins likes is pesto (recipe follows).

HARRY'S CIOPPINO

Seafood
3 pounds halibut, red snapper or sea bass cut
in good-sized chunks (halibut cheeks work
well)
1 large Dungeness crab or 2 lobster tails---
cooked
1 pint small clams or mussels---or a pint each
(you really can't have too much seafood in
this dish)
At least 1 pound jumbo shrimp
1 pound scallops

Sauce
3/4 cup olive oil, extra virgin
2 cups chopped sweet onion
1 cup chopped green pepper
4 cloves fresh garlic minced in the food
processor or shot through the garlic press
1 large can good quality tomatoes-preferably
plum tomatoes (chopped)
2 to 3 cups broth from the mollusks, plus 1
small can good minced clams and broth
2 cups fish stock made from bones, scraps and
the crab and lobster body shells
2 cups tomato juice (yes, really)
2 cups red wine
1/2 cup minced parsley (garnish)
1/2 to 1 cup Basil pesto

Seafood: Cut the fish into chunks, de-boning as
you go along. Crack the crab, peel the shrimp
and remove the black vein. Save the crab body

shell and the shrimp exoskeleton for the stock. Steam the mollusks in 2 cups of water until they open-remove top shells and save broth.

Sauce: Saute onion and pepper in olive oil until soft, add all other ingredients except parsley and cook ten minutes. Using a large kettle, arrange fish and shrimp in layers,cover with sauce and simmer on stove or in oven for 30 minutes. Add crab, lobster and mollusks and simmer 4 minutes.

Serve in deep bowls with shells and top with parsley. Serve with lots of crusty french or italian bread and put an extra plate at each setting for shells. I also serve this dish with cocktail forks and crab- or nutcrackers, to address the delicacy of eating crab, lobster and molluscs dripping with sauce.

Alternative method: Saute onion and pepper until soft and add all ingredients except parsley to a crock pot. Cook on high for 1 hour then simmer on low for 6 to 8 hours. Return to high setting, add fish and shrimp and cook for 30 minutes. Add lobster, crab and molluscs, wait 4 minutes and serve.

You can prepare this dish very nicely without the crab and lobster, just using fish shrimp and mollusks. I only add the crab and lobster for company, because the sauce and the french bread are really the meal. You can make it as basic as the beach or dress it up, but don't leave out the pesto---add more if you wish, but don't leave it out.

POTATO-PESTO SOUP #I

3 leeks or one bunch scallions
1/4 cup butter
3 cups finely diced potatoes (I use the food
    processor)
1 quart chicken or turkey broth
salt to taste (I <u>will</u> add salt to potato soup)
2 tablespoons butter
2 tablespoons flour
1/4 to 1/2 cup Green Peppercorn, Basil or Garlic
    Artichoke pesto

Wash and chop leeks or scallions and saute in 1/4 cup butter in a large skillet or heavy bottomed kettle for 5 minutes. Add the potatoes and broth, bring to just a boil and cook for 2 minutes. Reduce heat and simmer until the potatoes are tender. Scoop out vegetables with a slotted spoon and purée them in the blender or food mill and return to the broth. Melt the remaining butter and stir in flour. Add a cup of the broth mixture to the roux and stir until it thickens. Return to the kettle, add pesto to taste and let the soup come to a boil stirring constantly. Serve immediately in hot soup plates with crusty bread and a salad.

You may add cream or milk to this soup if desired. Of course I always go for the cream and add an extra day at the gym. I have discovered that exercise is a great equalizer in terms of eating whatever you want---within reason.

POTATO-PESTO SOUP #2

2 to 3 slices bacon
2 stalks celery finely chopped
1 small onion, finely chopped
3 medium potatoes peeled and diced---optional
1 cup chicken broth
1/2 teaspoon salt
2 tablespoons flour
2 cups milk
1/2 cup heavy cream---optional
1/4 to 1/2 cup Green Peppercorn, Basil or Garlic
    Artichoke pesto

If using bacon, cook until crisp and then remove from pan with a slotted spoon, or melt 1/4 cup of butter in a large skillet or kettle. Add vegetables and chicken broth, cover and cook for 15 minutes. Combine flour with a small amount of milk and add to potato mixture along with the rest of the milk. Cook over medium heat until the mixture boils, turn off heat and stir in pesto and cream. Garnish with bacon or parsley. Yes, I know all of the bad things about bacon, but I try to buy the nitrate-free brands and take some vitamin C to counteract the salt.

ARTICHOKE SOUP

1 can artichoke hearts, 8-1/2 ounce
1 medium potato peeled and diced
1 cup diced onion
1/4 cup butter
1/2 teaspoon salt
1 quart chicken broth
1/2 cup whipping cream
1/4 to 1/2 cup Artichoke, Basil, or Green
   Peppercorn pesto

Saute onions and potato in butter until translucent but not browned. Add half the artichokes, 2 cups chicken broth, cover and simmer for 15 minutes. Remove from heat and purée in blender or food mill. Return to kettle and add remaining artichokes (quartered or chopped), broth, pesto and cream. Heat through but do not boil. Garnish with parsley and serve with heated foccacia.

NEW AND IMPROVED TOMATO SOUP

When I was a child there were three foods which struck terror in my heart. Liver and onions, peanut butter and tomato soup. My mother, Nana, loved tomato soup.

NANA'S TOMATO SOUP, IMPROVED BY THE GENERATION GAP

In my mind, there is no way to improve liver and onions, even with pesto. However, seasoned with pesto, tomato soup can be manipulated into a good dish.

3 cups canned plum tomatoes or home-canned, if
    you have them
1 cup chicken or beef broth or bouillon
1 small onion diced very finely
1 teaspoon salt
1/2 teaspoon pepper
2 tablespoons Basil pesto
2 tablespoons butter
2 tablespoons flour
2 cups heavy cream or 1-1/2 cups milk and 1/2
    cup cream

Cook tomatoes, broth and seasonings in a kettle for thirty minutes then purée in a blender or food mill. Check the seasoning and see if you want to add more pesto. Melt the butter and stir in flour to make a paste which is then added to the tomato mixture. Add the milk or cream to the soup slowly to avoid curdling, return soup to heat and bring slowly to just below boiling and serve with bread and salad. Garnish with chopped parsley or croutons.

Notes:

SALADS

Victoria's Bella Cucina

The key to salads made with pesto is to put the pesto in the dressing. I do three basic dressings which work equally well for garden, vegetable or pasta salads. These dressings are a Pesto Vinaigrette, a Pesto Mayonnaise and a Creamy Pesto made with sour cream and mayonnaise. Feel free to change dressings for the salads--- with the exception of the seafood and turkey salads. I really think they are best when done with a creamy dressing. You may also use the plain pestos, although I usually only do this with the artichoke.

Do not substitute salad dressing for mayonnaise ---non, no, no!

PESTO VINAIGRETTE

1/3 cup wine vinegar or rice vinegar
2/3 cup olive oil
1 teaspoon salt---(optional; I don't use it)
1/2 teaspoon cracked pepper, black or mixed
1 to 2 tablespoons pesto, any flavor

I always double this recipe and keep it on hand.

Place all ingredients in a dressing bottle or a jar and shake before serving. Keep refrigerated.

For a creamier dressing, whirl the ingredients in a blender until the dressing appears opaque and thickened.

With the addition of a pesto to these recipes you can produce several different flavors depending on your pesto preference. Just add the pesto--- the other herbs are there.

PESTO MAYONNAISE

Emergency and Casual Gourmet Version

Add 1 to 2 tablespoons pesto to 1/2 cup prepared mayonnaise. Do not use salad dressing---only mayonnaise.

Homemade - Make Your Own

1 egg yolk
1/2 teaspoon dry mustard
1/4 teaspoon pepper
1 teaspoon lemon juice
1 cup light olive oil or salad oil
1/4 cup any green pesto or Garlic Artichoke

Process first 4 ingredients in blender, or whisk in a small bowl until mixture is blended well. Add the oil drop by drop whisking vigorously or blending until it begins to thicken and emulsify. Add the remaining oil in a steady stream and thin with more lemon juice if too thick. Beat in pesto at the very last and chill.

KEEP REFRIGERATED.

This is great with steamed artichokes and blanched asparagus or green beans.

CREAMY PESTO DRESSING

In this recipe you may substitute Quark or yogurt for the sour cream and imitation mayonnaise for the real stuff, if you are watching cholesterol.

1 cup sour cream
1/2 cup mayonnaise
1/2 cup any green or Garlic Artichoke pesto
milk or buttermilk to thin to your preference

Mix by hand and chill. Use as a dip or dressing. I'm going to count on you the reader to be able to put your own green salad together and use any of the above dressings to make it sing. However,....

My favorite green salads are very simple---I like buttercrunch lettuce and romaine for greens, fresh curly-leafed spinach if available. I use a few fresh sliced mushrooms, sweet red onion, a few chopped walnuts and homemade croutons---or a few tortellini or raditore *al dente*.

Check your area for a farmers market, even if you live in the city. Or make it an adventure in parking and go to the Pike Place Market. Going there can kill two birds with one stone.

DeLaurentis has wonderful crusty breads and an excellent selection of pastas, etc.

I use specific pasta for pasta salad, primarily because I want something that holds the sauce and looks interesting. I don't use the various vegetable pastas because I can't rely on what color they will be after cooking. Khaki pasta is not appealing. My favorite pasta is raditore, available in dry form from Antoine's at Larry's. I also like Del Verde bow ties, spirals and shells. There is excellent fresh pasta on the market now everywhere.

Pasta salads are the blank canvas of the kitchen to me---what do you like? I like mine to have contrasting textures--there is nothing more boring than having everything the same texture in a cold pasta salad. Here goes my version(s). I encourage you to modify any recipe in this book. The book should be considered just a launching pad and reference center---not "the book". I'm not an authority---I just like to play with food.

BASIC PASTA SALAD

2 to 3 cups dry pasta or 8 to 12 ounces fresh
pasta
3/4 cup mayonnaise, sour cream
1/2 cup pesto, cook's choice
sliced almonds
1/2 cup sliced water chestnuts or jicama
1/2 cup sliced sweet red pepper---or green
pepper, your choice
1 cup lightly steamed broccoli in small
flowerettes
1 cup artichoke hearts, canned or marinated
optional: Any baby vegetables, carrots, eggplant,
black olives (tasty, unless, of course, you hate
them), chopped scallions or red onion or
marinated brussel sprouts (keep an open
mind---Don't you remember the marinated
brussel sprouts from the salad bar? Not too
far removed from marinated artichoke hearts);
cubed cooked chicken, turkey or sliced italian
meats.

Mix mayonnaise with pesto and refrigerate to get
acquainted.

Cook pasta according to directions---yes, when
all else fails, I read the directions. For those of
you who bought bulk raditore---cook for ten
minutes in 3 quarts of boiling water plus 1
tablespoon of olive oil. Shells, bow ties and
spirals require eight to ten minutes. Pour cooked
pasta into a colander and rinse with cold water to
stop the cooking process. Place pasta in a large

bowl and add all other desired ingredients. Add the pesto mayonnaise and chill for one hour. Serve on a bed of lettuce with crusty bread.

This basic recipe can be varied according to the flavor of pesto used and your choice of meat or seafood. I love it with shrimp, crab and chicken, but it is also great with italian sausage or pepperoni. For a party where you are not familiar with the eating habits of all of the guests, safety dictates the chicken or turkey. Seafood can be a bit risky. While doing food demonstrations I run into many people who are allergic to shellfish. The last catered function I attended had a wonderful marinated calamari (squid), but I heard at least four people say they were allergic to shellfish.

The Sun-dried Tomato pesto tastes great with just pasta, marinated mushrooms, onion and italian sausage or pepperoni. Also great with calamari rings.

You can also use the pesto without mayonnaise if desired. I like the creaminess of the mayonnaise or sour cream, but prepare it both ways. Sometimes, the choice is made by my morning trip to the scale and whether or not it is a day to go to the gym.

RICE SALAD PESTO: Substitute rice for pasta in the previous recipe. You can also add a tablespoon of pesto to the water in which the rice is cooked, to add flavor.

LOBSTER SALAD WITH PESTO

Three 1-1/2 pound lobsters, or equivalent in
    tails (cooked, removed from shells and
    cooled)
1/2 cup pesto mayonnaise
3 tablespoons chopped scallions
3 tablespoons celery
tomato wedges and hard-boiled eggs to garnish

Cook and clean lobster---put them in boiling
water then simmer 10 minutes.

Mix mayonnaise, combine with lobster meat and
other ingredients, and top with tomato wedges
and eggs. You may add more mayonnaise if you
like.

Serve with lemon wedges.

There is a marvelous shrimp salad served at the
Royal Hawaiian Hotel in Honolulu. I do a
variation, and frequently add pesto to the
dressing ---you can do it with shrimp or add
several varieties of seafood. You can also go
with half seafood and half tortellini. Garlic
Artichoke pesto loves any kind of seafood.

SHRIMP OR SEAFOOD SALAD WITH PESTO

1 to 2 pounds cooked small or medium shrimp,
    crab or imitation crab
3/4 cup chopped celery
1/4 cup finely chopped scallions
1/2 cup slivered jicama, if desired
1/2 cup sliced black olives, if desired
1/2 cup slivered almonds, if desired (use 1/4
    cup in salad and rest for garnish)

Dressing
1/2 cup mayonnaise
1/2 cup sour cream
1/2 cup pesto (Basil, Garlic Artichoke or Green
    Peppercorn)

Mix dressing and place in refrigerator to chill.
You may use all mayonnaise if desired.

Place all other ingredients in a bowl and toss
with pesto dressing. Top with parsley garnish
and slivered almonds and serve hard rolls or
crusty bread.

PESTO POTATO SALAD

Just add a couple of tablespoons of Peppercorn,
Basil or Garlic Artichoke pesto to the dressing
for this american favorite.

PESTO CHICKEN OR TURKEY SALAD

3 cups cubed chicken or turkey
3/4 cup sliced celery
1/2 cup sliced black olives
1/4 cup chopped walnuts, pecans or pine nuts
1/4 cup slivered jicama, optional
1/4 cup chopped scallions

Dressing
1/2 cup mayonnaise
1/2 cup sour cream
1/2 cup pesto (Basil, Garlic Artichoke or Green Peppercorn)

Mix dressing and place in refrigerator to chill. You may use all mayonnaise if desired.

Place all other ingredients in a bowl and toss with pesto dressing. Top with parsley garnish and slivered almonds and serve hard rolls or crusty bread.

TOMATO AND PROVOLONE PESTO

Cooking is a recreational activity for me. One of the people with whom I really enjoy cooking is Michel Lalanne. He owns Michel's Antiques in Sun Valley and loves to cook and entertain, so his house and kitchen are designed around those activities. He doesn't measure--just makes it up as he goes along. Everything he serves is exquisite---except the goat cheese. There needs to be copious roasted garlic available for me to enjoy goat cheese.

Michel does a simple dish with tomatoes, thinly sliced provolone cheese, fresh Basil and vinaigrette; you can do it year-round with pesto.

You can also use slices of buffalo mozzarella---a semi-soft and delicious alternative. It's generally found in the deli cheese section of the market in a tub, or in specialty cheese shops.

1 or 2 large beefsteak tomatoes or several ripe
   plum tomatoes
1/2 pound thinly sliced provolone cut in halves
   or 8 ounces buffalo mozzarella sliced thinly
1 recipe vinaigrette
1/2 cup Basil, Green Peppercorn or Garlic
   Artichoke pesto

Layer tomatoes and thin slices of cheese in a shallow dish. Drizzle liberally with pesto and then cover with a well-shaken mixture of 1/3 cup wine or rice vinegar, 2/3 cup olive oil, 1 teaspoon salt (optional) and 1/4 teaspoon cracked black pepper. Marinate for one hour before serving. You can serve it immediately, but I like to give it some time.

I love this dish for brunch, lunch or dinner. It can also be a good appetizer served with crusty bread to dip in the oil. I personally really like the Colavita line of olive oils. They have a pepper olive oil that doesn't particularly go with pesto, but is a great oil for dipping.

BABY OR SLICED VEGETABLE SALAD

Lightly steam your favorite blend of baby vegetables or sliced standard vegetables. I do them in the microwave for 2 minutes on high in a shallow dish. This makes them tender yet still crunchy enough to constitute salad fare. Rinse under cold water to halt the cooking process and drain. Toss with any of the pesto dressings and serve as a side dish.

Notes:

Notes:

PESTO & VEGETABLES

Victoria's Bella Cucina

I am addicted to two things: butter and garlic. I can work on the butter addiction by substituting pesto and still get my garlic fix. The various pestos are wonderful for people who must watch their cholesterol and salt and are a good way to spice up traditional vegetable dishes for yourself or company.

I use the microwave to steam all of my vegetables except artichokes. With artichokes I still prefer to risk my life using Nana's pressure cooker. Barbara Kafka's Microwave Gourmet has a great section on preparing vegetables in the microwave. As a general rule I use a very shallow dish, I use 1 to 2 tablespoons of water or white wine, cover with plastic wrap, perforate the plastic wrap with a knife and cook for 4 minutes. Summer squash and mushrooms cook in 3 minutes and baked potatoes come in at 9 minutes. I prefer to start my potatoes in the microwave for 3 to 4 minutes---then they're off for a half hour in the real oven. There is simply no comparison in the quality of a potato skin---traditional oven versus microwave---even if you give your potato skin to the dog.

STEAMED VEGETABLES WITH PESTO

Prepare your favorite vegetable or combination of vegetables in the microwave or stovetop steamer. Add 1 to 2 tablespoons of pesto and toss lightly. Serve immediately. Sprinkle a small amount of parmesan cheese on top for garnish.

I prefer the green pestos for vegetables, except with green beans, eggplant and zucchini. These work well with the Sun-dried Tomato.

I sometimes toss leftover pasta spirals or shells with vegetables, just for a little texture differentiation---to see if the kids will respond any differently.

GREEN BEANS
WITH PESTO AND BACON

Toss cooked green beans with 1/4 cup chopped walnuts, 3 strips of bacon, crisp and crumbled, and 2 tablespoons of pesto; cooks' choice.

Other Examples:
carrots or green beans with Basil or Garlic
    Artichoke pesto
any vegetable with Green Peppercorn pesto
mushrooms sauted, then tossed lightly with any
    of the green pestos
summer squashes with any of the greens
cooked tomatoes with Basil pesto
fresh limas with greens or red pesto
corn on the cob with pesto butter or plain red
    pesto

creamed onions mixed with 2 tablespoons of any
green pesto
asparagus or leeks with Green Peppercorn or
Garlic Artichoke
spaghetti squash with Basil, Peppercorn or red
pesto

***MUSHROOMS, CAULIFLOWER OR
BRUSSEL SPROUTS STEAMED FOR 1
MINUTE AND THEN MARINATED IN ANY
GREEN PESTO VINAIGRETTE---delicious as
appetizers, salad or pasta additions

NEW POTATOES MCMILLIAN

When I first met Dick McMillian he had never
tasted pesto, but he has a keen sense of
adventure and knows more than just the
Backyard Gourmet Barbecue Sauce that made
him famous. I brought him samples of all of the
pestos and for a week I got a wake-up call each
morning so that Dick could tell me how he used
pesto the night before. He really likes new
potatoes tossed with a little butter and pesto
instead of parsley. Pesto truly is a multiple
seasoning and you just get more flavor when you
use it.

Steam enough new potatoes to feed your family
or guests. This will vary based on the size of
the potatoes---here we get them varying from the
size of pecans to the size of plum tomatoes. I
really like the small ones best---figure a small

handful per person and be overjoyed if you can saute leftovers for breakfast the next morning. Add Basil, dill, Peppercorn, or Garlic Artichoke pesto to taste (1/4 cup for 4 persons) and toss lightly. Add a little butter if desired.

Please don't be intimidated by the word "steam." If you want to boil those potatoes or cook them in your pressure cooker, do it. Modify the recipes in this book to coincide with your comfort zone in the kitchen. Michel Lalanne does not own a microwave and he is a superb cook.

BAKED POTATOES PESTO PESTO

The baked potato is a marvelous vehicle for condiments and can be stretched to a meal without much work. Pesto is a natural with baked potatoes, and again, a good choice for those who must watch cholesterol and sodium.

To pesto a baked potato, simply bake it, open it and add pesto. My favorite is with the Sun-dried Tomato and the Green Peppercorn, but the Garlic Artichoke is a subtle sleeper in this race.

Garlic Artichoke is so tasty that all the men I know simply eat it with a spoon---some while sitting in the bathtub.

I use 1 tablespoon of pesto per medium sized potato, and since I make a great many evening meals out of baked potatoes, I generally add jack, mozzarella or cheddar cheese and stick it under the broiler to melt---it can also be done in the microwave, but I like my cheese bubbly and brown---and because I'm so fussy about the potato skin the conventional oven is already hot.

You know that recipe that has you carefully measure out three or four herbs to add---and you have only one of them in your spice drawer. One tablespoon of pesto gives you the best of several herbs plus garlic. Start thinking about pesto in terms of a seasoning. Again, it will be an arsenal of fresh herbs in your refrigerator or freezer---no more snipping, washing and babying plants through the winter.

POTATOES PESTO AU GRATIN

Nana always teased me about potatoes au gratin. As a three-year old I mispronounced au gratin as hog rotten and it became one of the favorite family dinner party reminders---especially polished and presented to new dates. Potatoes au gratin are still a favorite of mine and I fix them often. I do use butter, and sometimes I use cream instead of milk. I used to add chives and other herbs, but now I just add pesto and cheese.

Bake one potato per person---in the real oven; you need crisp skins for this dish.

When potatoes are done, cut into halves, remove the pulp to a mixing bowl and save the skins. Add a tablespoon of Peppercorn, Basil or Garlic Artichoke pesto for each potato, a teaspoon of butter for each potato and add enough milk or cream to whip to a nice light consistency.

Fill skins with potato-pesto mixture and top with your favorite cheese: Mozzarella, jack or cheddar. I also sprinkle a bit of grated parmesan and paprika on top. Place potato halves on a cookie sheet 5 inches from a pre-heated broiler. Broil until cheese bubbles and is slightly brown on top; brush with pesto and serve.

VICKI JO'S FAVORITE HOG ROTTEN POTATO

My best potato these days is the above recipe prepared with Garlic Artichoke or Peppercorn pesto and about a tablespoon of smoked salmon per potato. Mix the smoked salmon in with the potato mixture and proceed as above. In Sequim, we have Alder Springs Smoked Salmon and it is my favorite, but I can't forgive Del for shutting down Bandit's Pizza parlor and depriving me of my favorite comfort food---the Bandit Bunkhouse Sandwich---turkey, ham, bacon, lettuce and tomato on toasted sourdough---great. Besides smoked salmon,

Alder Springs has a wonderful line of smoked
turkey, baby back ribs, *et cetera*, and they do
mail order.

SCALLOPED POTATOES PESTO

4 to 5 medium potatoes, peeled and cut into
  1/8 inch slices
1/2 cup pesto plus extra for the top when done
milk, half and half or cream
grated cheddar, gruyere, swiss or jack cheese
  (lowfat is fine)
1 sliced sweet onion---optional

Peel and slice potatoes and soak in cold water
for thirty minutes. Drain in colander and then
dry on absorbent toweling. Spray 9 x 9 x 3 pan
with olive oil mist or Pam. In the pan alternate
layers of potato with onion and cheese. Season
each layer with cracked or ground pepper. Dot
the top layer with butter and add milk mixed
with pesto to barely cover potatoes.

Bake at 350° for 50 minutes or until potatoes are
tender but not soft and mushy. Drizzle 2
tablespoons of pesto mixed with 2 tablespoons
melted butter or olive oil over top and serve.
Suggested pestos are Basil, Garlic Artichoke and
Peppercorn. A little cheese on the top doesn't
hurt---then drizzle with pesto.

62 VEGETABLES

Notes:

PASTA

Victoria's Bella Cucina

Pesto is traditionally a sauce for pasta. For the classic approach combine any pesto, red or green, with any pasta. Top with parmesan cheese and serve. This will always underscore your genius in the kitchen. Thus, we move to variations on a theme: Look at the section end for **pesto pizzas**.

PASTA WITH BACON AND BASIL

1/2 pound lean bacon (preferably nitrate free),
  finely chopped, cooked and drained
1/4 cup butter
1 onion in thin slices
1 cup sliced mushrooms
1 large can plum tomatoes, chopped
3/4 cup dry white wine
2 cups dry pasta---raditore, spirals or bows
1/4 to 1/2 cup Basil pesto

Saute onion, mushrooms in butter for 3 to 4 minutes. Add wine, tomatoes, bacon and pesto and simmer for 15 minutes. Serve over cooked pasta and top with 1/2 cup of grated parmesan, romano or asiago cheese.

Asiago is a cheese very similar to parmesan and a reasonable substitute. Many cooks prefer it.

BASIL TOMATO SAUCE

1/4 cup olive oil
2 onions sliced (thinly)
1 large carrot peeled and sliced
1 one pound can plum tomatoes--you can use
    the others in an emergency, but the plum
    tomatoes have better body, flavor and color
1 small can tomato paste or purée
1/2 cup water
1/2 cup red wine
pinch oregano
1/2 cup Basil pesto
extra garlic always welcomed

Saute onions and garlic with oil in saucepan.
Add remaining ingredients and simmer on low
heat or in crockpot on high for four hours. If
you want a smooth sauce you can run it through
the food mill or blender at hour three. I just run
the tomatoes through the blender before adding
and let it cook.

Serve with pasta.

FUSS-FREE MARINARA SAUCE

1/2 cup chopped onion
1/4 cup olive oil
4 cups canned plum tomatoes
1/2 to 1 cup Basil pesto
pinch oregano

extra garlic always welcomed

Saute onion and garlic in oil. Add all other ingredients and simmer uncovered until desired thickness---about an hour, or a little more if you add the 1/2 cup of red wine which I feel is absolutely necessary.

Serve with pasta.

FENNEL-FLAVORED RED SAUCE FOR PASTA

2 large cans plum tomatoes---run through a
    food mill or quick cycle in the blender or
    food processor
1/4 cup olive oil
2 to 3 pounds sweet italian sausage
2 pounds mushrooms, sliced
1 large onion sliced thinly
1 cup red wine
1/2 cup Basil pesto
1/2 cup Sun-dried Tomato pesto
    (contains fennel)
3 tablespoons butter

Saute onions, sausage and mushrooms in oil. Remove from pan with slotted spoon and discard oil. Combine with other ingredients except butter, in a large saucepan or crockpot. Simmer on low heat for three hours. Crockpot users: go with high heat for three hours or low heat all

day. Add butter just prior to serving and mix
well.

Serve Fennel-Flavored Red Sauce over pasta
with freshly grated parmesan or romano cheese.

PESTO LASAGNA
WITH CHICKEN OR TURKEY

2 sheets fresh lasagna---spinach, if you can find
    it, or 1 package dry lasagna prepared
    according to directions
1/2 pound sliced mushrooms
1 cup cooked chicken or turkey
1/2 cup fresh lemon juice
1-1/2 cups chicken broth
3/4 cup milk
1/3 cup butter
1/4 cup flour
1 onion, finely chopped
1 egg
1 cup any green pesto or the Artichoke
1 cup sour cream
1 cup grated parmesan, asiago or romano

Melt half the butter and saute onion until soft.
Stir in flour and cook for a minute then
gradually add the chicken broth and milk and
bring to a boil, stirring constantly. Remove from
heat and add pesto and chopped chicken or
turkey.

Spread one third of the sauce in the bottom of a greased lasagna pan and alternate three layers of pasta and sauce. Finish with a layer of pasta. Use remaining butter and the lemon juice to saute mushrooms lightly. Spread mushrooms on top of the lasagna and cover with a mixture of sour cream beaten with the egg. Sprinkle with cheese and bake at 375° for 35 minutes.

LASAGNA VARIATIONS

This recipe is also good done with crab, shrimp or smoked salmon. Just substitute your favorite in this category for the 1 cup of chicken or turkey.

I do a variation of a classic meat lasagna using a couple of different options. I confess to really liking the cheese-laden varieties and I do them with both the red and green pestos.

1. I like to use seafood for the sauce, and add the mushrooms directly to the sauce---I make the white sauce as in the preceding recipe and add the seafood and pesto to it. I then alternate layers of sauce, pasta, sauce, shredded mozzarella cheese, pasta, sauce, cheese and ending with cheese. Into the oven at 375° for 35 minutes.

2. I make the seafood sauce, add the mush-rooms to it and use ricotta then mozzarella until the top layer. The top layer is ricotta beaten

with an egg and topped with a liberal cup of shredded mozzarella and 1/2 cup of parmesan.

3. I make a meat sauce using the same amounts of onion and mushrooms sauted together with italian sausage. I combine this with 1 cup of Sun-dried Tomato pesto and 1-1/2 cups of tomato sauce or chopped plum tomatoes in juice. You can also use 1/2 cup of the Basil pesto and 2 cups of tomatoes or tomato sauce added to the meat. Layer as in the previous two versions and top with ricotta egg mixture, mozzarella and parmesan.

You can mix 1/2 Sun-dried Tomato pesto with 1/2 tomato sauce and add Italian sausage or seafood for a dynamite red sauce for lasagna.

PASTA AND MUSHROOM SAUCE

Saute 2 cups of sliced mushrooms in 2 tablespoons of butter. Make a basic bechamel sauce adding another tablespoon of butter to mushrooms, along with 2 tablespoons flour and 1 cup of milk. Add 1/2 to 1 cup of green pesto and 1/2 cup of cream and serve over Antoine's Raditore, fresh raditore or other pasta. Garnish with sliced almonds, fresh parsley or parmesan cheese.

REMEMBER THAT THE MEAT AND SEAFOOD SECTIONS HAVE SEVERAL

GOOD RECIPES THAT ARE MADE WITH
PASTA. SCALLOPS AND SHRIMP PESTO
AND THE SEAFOOD SAUTE ARE THE
QUICKEST AND BEST PASTA DISHES I
KNOW OF. DON'T FORGET TO THUMB
THROUGH BOTH SECTIONS WHEN YOU
ARE THINKING ABOUT PASTA AND
PESTO FOR TONIGHT.

PASTA AND CHICKEN SCALLOPS

Cook 2 cups of ditali or orzo. While pasta is
cooking saute 1 finely chopped onion, 4 slices of
chopped bacon and 1/2 pound of fresh
mushrooms. When bacon is crisp add 8 ounces
of cooked chopped chicken. Drain cooked pasta
thoroughly and mix with meat/mushroom
mixture, adding 1/2 to 1 cup of pesto and 1 cup
of heavy cream. Place in scallop shells, sprinkle
with 1/2 cup bread crumbs and 1/2 cup gruyere
cheese evenly divided amongst filled shells.
Dish may also be done in an a casserole or au
gratin pan.

PASTA AND SHRIMP

Use your favorite shaped pasta for this one. I've
made it with several different shapes and I think
I like raditore or gemelli the best---it just holds
sauce and flavor better than any of the others.

Put 2 cups of radiatore on to cook for 8 to 10 minutes. Saute 1/2 pound of mushrooms and 1/2 pound of shelled shrimp in 1/4 cup of butter. Here's a choice. Make 3 cups of bechamel sauce and add a cup of green pesto, or add 1 cup of Sun-dried Tomato to 3 cups of tomato sauce and add whichever one you have prepared to the shrimp and mushroom mixture. Toss with cooked pasta and serve with parmesan sprinkled on top.

DOCK PASTA WITH PESTO

Cook 2 cups of radiatore or 1-1/2 cups of good quality elbow macaroni. Always add a little olive oil to the water when cooking pasta to keep it from sticking together---a tablespoon should do it.

Melt 2 tablespoons of butter in a pan and stir in a 1/2 cup of light cream a tablespoon of grated lemon rind, 1/2 pound shrimp and 3 tablespoons of green pesto. Add drained pasta to pan and toss. Heat through, place on a platter or large pasta dish and garnish with fresh parsley and parmesan cheese.

You know what to serve with all of these pasta dishes, right? Salad and crusty bread.

MOST OF THE SAUCES IN THIS SECTION
CAN BE USED WITH FETTUCINE AND
LINGUINE. ALSO GOOD, ARE RAVIOLI
AND TORTELLINI. THINK ABOUT THE
SAUCE AND HOW YOU WANT TO SERVE
IT AND AS WE USED TO SAY IN
PRE-SCHOOL, "PICK YOUR CHOOSE."

The emergency gourmet mixes 1/2 cup of Sun-
dried Tomato pesto, 1/2 cup red wine with a jar
of bottled red sauce. Instant success!

PESTO AND PASTA PIE

3/4 cup vermicelli
3 tablespoons olive oil
5 large eggs, well beaten
1 thinly sliced onion
1 cup sliced mushrooms
1 package frozen spinach thawed and drained,
    or 12 ounces cooked fresh spinach, cooled
    and drained
1/4 pound cream cheese
3/4 cup half and half
2 tablespoons Basil or other green pesto
1/4 cup grated parmesan or romano
artichoke hearts, if desired

Cook pasta for 2 minutes, drain and mix with
two of the beaten eggs, 1 tablespoon olive oil
and 2 tablespoons of fresh parsley (or substitute
more pesto here).

Press the noodle mixture into a 9 inch pie plate or flan dish, also covering the sides. Cover the rim of the pasta with foil and bake at 375° for 10 minutes.

While the "crust" is cooking, saute the onion and mushrooms in the remaining oil. Remove from heat and mix with spinach. Beat the cream cheese and pesto with the remaining 3 eggs, combine with the spinach mixture and spread evenly in the pasta "crust". Sprinkle grated cheese on the top and bake for 25 minutes or until a knife blade inserted in the middle of the pie comes out clean and the filling is set. Serve warm with additional pesto for the top.

REMEMBER THAT YOU CAN ADD THE GREEN PESTOS TO ALMOST ANY CREAM SAUCE AND YOU CAN ADD THE RED, BASIL AND GARLIC ARTICHOKE TO ALMOST ANY RED SAUCE. TRY THE SAUCES WITH SEAFOOD CANNELLONI. TRY THEM WITH CRAB, SHRIMP AND CHEESE. EXPERIMENT! EXPERIMENT! EXPERIMENT!

PESTO WALNUT SAUCE

I prefer walnuts to pine nuts in pesto because often pine nuts will register as bitter. Walnuts are also only a fraction of the cost. Don't be brow-beaten into doing "the classic italian thing".

The critical issue today is not how "classic" a dish is created or remains, but rather how it tastes. A case in point---Haggis---apologies to my family, still pretending to enjoy this dish in Scotland.

Melt 1/2 cup of butter in a non-stick pan with 1/2 cup of any green pesto---I like Basil, Artichoke and Green Peppercorn the best. Saute for 1 minute then add 1/3 cup chicken broth and 1/3 cup parmesan cheese.

Drain cooked pasta and mix with 1/4 cup butter and 1/2 cup sour cream. Serve in pasta bowls topped with Pesto Walnut Sauce. Pistachios or hazelnuts can be tasty too.

PASTA WITH KIDNEY BEANS

1-1/2 cups fettucine or raditore
1 15 ounce can kidney beans
1/4 cup pesto, red or green
6 tablespoons olive oil
1/2 pound diced mozzarella cheese
a pinch chili powder

Cook pasta with a tablespoon of oil until *al dente*. Simultaneously heat remaining oil in non-stick pan and add pesto, chili powder and kidney beans. Heat through gently. Drain cooked pasta and stir in hot mixture. Stir in diced mozzarella, which will start to melt somewhat on the way to the table.

PASTA WITH POTATOES

2 medium basic firm-flesh potatoes, peeled and
    sliced thinly
8 ounces fresh fettucine
1 tablespoon olive oil
1/4 cup butter
2 tablespoons green pesto
1 tablespoon poppy seeds or 1/2 cup chopped
    walnuts

Cook potatoes until tender, but still holding their
shape. Cook fettucine until *al dente*. Drain both
thoroughly and toss with pesto, butter and poppy
seeds or nuts.

PIZZA

Pizza isn't really pasta, but here it is anyway.

Pesto has become a popular addition to pizza in
the last few years. Make the powerful G.A.S.P.
pizza a must (garlic, artichokes, sun-dried
tomatoes and pesto) at the famous Romio's.
Then drive to Sequim and try the pesto pizzas at
Pizza Primo.

Here are a few versions for you to try at home---
with a prepared crust or your recipe.

Mix one 8 ounce tub of Sun-dried Tomato pesto with an equal amount of tomato sauce and use in lieu of pizza sauce---add your favorite toppings.

Use the above sauce, add artichoke hearts, slivered garlic and cheese---bake and add a teaspoon of Basil pesto to each slice after cutting. Putting the pesto in the center of the pie makes a nice presentation.

For those who like the full flavor of the Sun-dried Tomato pesto, try making a pizza with full-strength Sun-dried Tomato as the sauce and top the pizza with slivered garlic and goat cheese.

Spread Basil pesto on a pizza crust. Add mushrooms, onion, olives, cheese, sausage or pepperoni and bake. Garnish with fresh chopped tomatoes.

Spread Garlic Artichoke pesto on a pizza crust. Add mushrooms, olives, onions, cheese and seafood. Bake and garnish with fresh chopped tomatoes. In an emergency, just spread pesto on a Boboli crust, add cheese and run it under the broiler.

76 PASTA

Notes:

SEAFOOD

Victoria's Bella Cucina

WHITE FISH

Marinate any white fish, tuna or swordfish in the
marinade presented below above and serve in the
same manner. Try marinated red snapper.

My friend Steve bakes firm whitefish with a thin
layer of Artichoke pesto and a squeeze of lemon
---top with parmesan if desired.

PESTO MARINADE

2 tablespoons pesto
1/4 cup wine
1/4 cup olive oil

HALIBUT PESTO

1. Marinate in pesto marinade using Basil,
Garlic Artichoke or Green Peppercorn pesto for
the base. Broil or barbecue and serve remaining
sauce melted on top of steaks or filets. I really
prefer filets, since the steaks can sometimes be
very dry. I usually just buy a halibut roast and
filet it myself, using the bones and scraps to
make fish broth to stick in the freezer and use
for cioppino.

2. Bake halibut steaks or filets in 3/4 cup of
white wine at 350° for about 20 minutes. Brush
tops of steaks with Green Peppercorn, Basil or

Garlic Artichoke pesto and return to oven for five minutes. Serve with pan juices and wedges of lemon or lime.

BAKED FISH WITH TARRAGON ALMOND STUFFING

3/4 cup butter
1/4 cup chopped onion
1/2 cup sliced mushrooms
1/2 cup celery
3 cups soft bread crumbs
3 eggs, lightly beaten
1/2 cup Tarragon pesto (special order)
1/2 cup chopped almonds
5 to 7 pound whole red snapper, cleaned, washed
    and dried

Saute onion and mushrooms in 1/4 cup butter until tender. Add breadcrumbs, celery, eggs, almonds and pesto. Mix well and stuff fish. Sew the fish closed---large needle, coarse thread (white).

Melt remaining butter. Place fish in a foil lined baking dish and brush with butter and place in a pre-heated 400° oven. Bake for an hour and 15 minutes or until fish flakes easily with a fork. Baste often with remaining butter, and I usually add a teaspoon of pesto to the basting butter.

SOLE ROLL-UPS

8 dover sole filets
1/4 pound crab or shrimp meat
3/4 cup shredded jack cheese
1/2 cup Sun-dried Tomato pesto or green pesto
3/4 cup white wine, plus 1 tablespoon pesto

Overlap two sole filets, end to end. Spread each set of filets with 2 tablespoons of pesto. At one end place 1/4 of the crab or shrimp, 1/4 of the cheese. Roll tightly and secure with toothpicks.

Place in small roasting dish and pour pesto/wine mixture over the rolled filets. Bake at 400° for fifteen minutes, serve with pan juices and wedges of lemon or lime.

If you would like a cream sauce: while the sole is cooking in the oven make a standard bechamel sauce. Melt 2 tablespoons of butter in a pan and mix in 2 tablespoons of flour. Add one cup of cold milk and stir until mixture thickens. Add 1/4 cup pesto, or pesto to taste and pour over sole when done.

Every time I make a cream sauce, I think of Miss Finney, a former home economics teacher at Vashon High School. The cream sauce is the only thing we made in that class that I have ever replicated. The other two things I distinctly remember were fondant and **welsh rarebit**. I haven't had to prepare either although welsh rarebit could benefit from a bit of pesto.

FRESH TROUT

Fresh trout are wonderful on their own, but they are also good with pesto.

I clean them, and because I don't like to look at their eyes, I generally remove the head at the gills, but leave the tail. The tail is a critical part of de-boning cooked trout. The waitress will bone it for you at the Pine Tavern in Bend, Oregon and the Lodge Dining room in Sun Valley, Idaho. At home, you need all the help you can get with this process, so leave the tail on.

I sometimes saute the trout in a little butter and Garlic Artichoke pesto and serve with steamed vegetables and a salad. I use 1 tablespoon of butter and 1 tablespoon of pesto in a non-stick pan. Yes, you can use a heavy cast iron skillet if you like, but non-stick is easy to clean.

Sometimes I slather the inside and outside of the trout in pesto and bake them quickly in a 400° oven.

I also really like trout done on the barbecue or camp fire grill, served with pesto butter brushed or poured on the top.

Try the Basil, Peppercorn and Garlic Artichoke pestos. Try the same techniques for cooking and seasoning **sea bass** and **catfish**.

SALMON

Salmon is a Northwest specialty which satisfies almost anyone. It stands well on its own, poached, baked, barbecued or sauted. For a change of pace try it with pesto or one of the pesto sauces described in the **Salad** and **Appetizer** sections.

The green pestos are wonderful for salmon, as a marinade, baste, condiment or sauce. My favorite dish is salmon with hollandaise, but I'm lazy and I also like a bechamel with pesto or an alfredo with pesto on salmon. My favorite pestos for salmon are Green Peppercorn, Garlic Artichoke and Tarragon.

SALMON WITH
PESTO BECHAMEL SAUCE

We're not going to burden you with any of that constant reference stuff, i.e., asking to incorporate "Mary Beth's special stock" or "sauce from Page 33". I hate that. Not only do you need to jockey back and forth in the book, but Mary Beth's special doodah sauce or stock usually is made with at least three things that aren't available in my kitchen at the time the deed needs to be done. Finally, it is an hour prior to the ETA of my dinner guests and I don't have time to run to the store or simmer something for three hours, then clarify it. I'm

not patient, my hair is generally on fire and I
want whatever right now.

Poach salmon in white wine or bake in at 425°
for 15 to 20 minutes depending on size of steaks
or filets.

While the salmon is cooking, make a basic
bechamel. Melt 2 tablespoons of butter in a
non-stick pan and add 2 tablespoons of flour,
mixing to a paste. Add 1 cup of milk all at once
and stir continuously (use a whisk) until mixture
thickens. Add 1/2 cup of pesto and serve over
cooked salmon garnished with fresh chopped
parsley.

BAKED OR POACHED SALMON
SERVED CHILLED
WITH PESTO SAUCE

1 whole 4 to 5 pound salmon--cleaned, head and
  tail intact
Wine for poaching, if this is the method of
  choice

Poach or bake salmon. Chill and serve
garnished with a ring of lemon slices and pesto
sauce on the side. For the pesto sauce mix 1
part pesto to two parts sour cream, yogurt or a
combination of sour cream and mayonnaise.
Basil, Green Peppercorn or Garlic Artichoke
suggested.

SALMON CROQUETTES

If you have any salmon left over from the above, you can make cold salmon sandwiches with cream cheese and pesto---or you can make croquettes.

1 pound cooked, flaked salmon or canned
    salmon (good quality)
3/4 cup bread crumbs
1/2 cup minced onion
1/2 cup real mayonnaise
1 egg
1/2 cup green pesto---Garlic Artichoke, Basil,
    Peppercorn or Tarragon
vegetable or olive oil for frying

Mix salmon with 1/2 cup bread crumbs and other ingredients and shape in 2 inch patties. Coat patties with remaining bread crumbs. Heat oil in a large skillet on medium and cook the patties until browned and crisp, turning only once. Drain patties on a paper towel and keep warm in the oven until finished.

Serve with pesto mayonnaise or pesto sauce.

SALMON PESTO ALFREDO

This is for the emergency gourmet.

Cook salmon as above. Add 1/2 cup pesto to 1 cup of alfredo sauce from the deli. Heat through and serve over salmon with chopped parsley as garnish.

SHELLFISH

CALAMARI STEAKS

4 medium calamari (squid) steaks (they really are shellfish)

Marinate calamari steaks in pesto marinade for 1/2 to 1 hour then barbecue, broil or flash-saute. If you barbecue or broil serve remaining sauce over steaks. If you flash-saute, add some of the marinade to the pan, simmer until reduced and thickened, add a few tablespoons of cream and serve on top of steaks.

SHRIMP OR PRAWNS PESTO

Prepare as for above using medium shrimp or prawns which have been shelled and deveined. Saute shrimp briefly in butter and pesto, add mushrooms and cook until shrimp turn pink, add 1/2 cup white wine and simmer until slightly thicker. Serve with crusty bread or pour over cooked pasta.

Both of these dishes can be prepared in the microwave by mixing all ingredients together, pouring in a shallow dish, covering with plastic wrap and cooking according to your microwave directions for seafood and shellfish. I generally use the smaller scallops and they take about one minute in the mikey.

Be certain to perforate plastic wrap to vent steam. Scallops may make a popping sound when cooking---don't panic.

SHRIMP TARRAGON

16 to 20 large raw shrimp, peeled and deveined
1/2 cup melted butter
2 tablespoons minced fresh onion or scallion
1 cup sliced mushrooms
1/2 cup Tarragon pesto (special order)
1 cup dry white wine

Rinse cleaned shrimp and place in a shallow baking dish. Saute onion and mushrooms lightly in butter. Toss with pesto and spoon mixture on shrimp. Pour wine over shrimp and mushroom mixture. Bake 10 to 12 minutes until shrimp are pink. Baste twice. Serve with fresh lemon. Try **Shrimp Tarragon** with 1/2 cup of vermouth instead of the wine. Cook for three minutes in the microwave on full power. Serve over rice or pasta. May also be served as an appetizer with french bread.

RED SHRIMP OR PRAWNS

Prepare as for above using Sun-dried Tomato pesto mixed with a little olive oil to thin it. Use a red table wine instead of white wine. This is best done as a saute.

SCALLOPS PESTO

Saute scallops and one cup sliced mushrooms quickly in 2 tablespoons of butter and 1/4 cup of Basil, Garlic Artichoke, Tarragon or Green Peppercorn pesto. Add 1/2 cup of white wine, heat through and simmer until slightly thickened. Serve scallops in bowls with crusty french or italian bread or pour over cooked pasta.

MUSSELS

Of the bi-valve family, mussels are my favorite ---especially Penn Cove mussels. They have a distinctly delicate flavor and are a fun food to serve and eat---isn't that what it's all about? Scrub and de-beard enough mussels to feed your crowd. Steam in a large kettle with fresh water (or white wine) and garlic until they pop open.

Remove to large serving dishes and serve with melted pesto butter and lemon slices. I like to do this family style with a baguette, or other crusty bread, to catch drips.

Try adding any flavor pesto to the water for steaming. I suggest 1/4 cup of the green pestos. Some coarsely diced tomatoes and onions make a nice addition, creating a little color and more flavor.

Another way to prepare mussels is to steam them in white wine and garlic. When open, remove to a warm dish and add cream, fresh lemon juice, coarsely chopped tomatoes and a couple of tablespoons of pesto to the broth and heat through. Pour over mussels and serve. The broth is delicious and begs to be consumed with crusty bread or baguettes.

When eating mussels---use your cocktail fork to get the first one, then use that shell to pick and place the remaining mussels in your mouth---this gives you that sticky fingered, real interaction with the food. Use good bread to mop up.

CLAMS WITH PESTO

Clams love pesto. Steam clams in fresh water
and garlic until they open, and serve with melted
pesto butter.

Remove the top shell from butter clams and
saute for two minutes in 1 tablespoon of butter
and 1 tablespoon of pesto. Serve on the half
shell with lemon wedges or alone.

PINK SCALLOPS

I like to serve pink scallops because the shell
color makes such a nice presentation. Pink
scallops need to be cooked or flash frozen the
day they are caught, but they are exquisite food
for the soul. Scrub the scallops and steam until
they open in fresh water and garlic, with perhaps
a sprig of Rosemary or a tablespoon of Garlic
Artichoke pesto. Serve with melted pesto butter.

OYSTERS

Oysters go well with the green pestos in any
form. You can even add a 1/2 cup of pesto to
your oyster stew---if you like oyster stew.

OYSTERS "T"

Around here we get lots of fresh oysters and the preferred method of cooking is on a bonfire with a grate at the beach. Place cleaned oysters on a barbecue grate until they open. Serve with plain pesto or keep a pot of melted pesto butter on the grill. All of the greens are excellent.

Place oysters, sans top shells, on the barbecue and brush with melted pesto butter as a baste. Serve with melted pesto butter, crusty bread and a green salad.

If you want to do oysters on the half shell you can pan-saute them the same way Chiquita does her butter clams. Remove the top shells and saute for 2 to 3 minutes (depending on the size of the oyster) in 1 tablespoon butter and 1 tablespoon of any of the green pestos.

Note: I'm not fond of oysters. However, my oyster of choice is the small Quilcene oyster---with lots of seasoning to hide the texture!!!

SCALLOPED OYSTERS

1/2 cup butter
1-1/2 cups rolled cracker crumbs
1-1/2 pints small Quilcene oysters
1/2 cup oyster juice
1/2 cup heavy cream
2 tablespoons any green pesto
buttered breadcrumbs

Spray a 1-1/2 quart baking dish with Pam and cover with a layer of cracker crumbs. Add a layer of oysters and another of cracker crumbs. Dot with butter and make another layer of oysters and crumbs, dotted with butter. Mix pesto, cream and oyster juices and pour over the top covering with buttered bread crumbs. Bake in a 400° oven for 25 minutes.

Raw oysters (Yuk!) can be served with pesto in lieu of hot sauce.

THE DEVIL'S OYSTERS

1 pint Quilcene oysters (small), cleaned and
    chopped
1/2 cup minced onion
1/2 cup chopped mushrooms
1/4 cup butter
3 tablespoons flour
1/2 cup half and half
1 teaspoon dry mustard

1 teaspoon White Wine Worcestershire
Crystal Hot Sauce or Tabasco to taste
1/2 to 1 cup green pesto
an egg yolk, beaten
1/4 cup bread crumbs
1/4 cup parmesan cheese

Pre-heat oven to 400°. Saute onion and
mushrooms in butter for two minutes. Add flour
and cream---cook until thickened. Add oysters,
seasonings and pesto and simmer for a minute.
Stir in egg yolk and mix well---turn into scallop
shells or small shallow dishes and cover with
bread crumbs and cheese.

Bake 15 minutes and serve with salad and bread.

Notes:

92 SEAFOOD

Notes:

POULTRY

Victoria's Bella Cucina

BOBBY WEIR'S CHICKEN
. WITH POLENTA

This dish may be made with selected chicken
parts or the whole bird, cut into serving size
pieces.

4 chicken breasts or one frying chicken cut into
    pieces
2 cups sliced or a half pound small button
    mushrooms
1/2 cup chopped onions
3 cups canned tomatoes with juice
1/2 cup red table wine
1/2 cup Basil, Sun-dried Tomato pesto
olive oil
1 recipe polenta

Saute chicken in a large fry pan or heavy kettle
with a bit of olive oil until lightly browned.
Add mushrooms and onions and saute for 2
minutes. Add tomatoes, wine and pesto to the
chicken and simmer for 50 minutes while polenta
is baking. When polenta is done, serve with
chicken and sauce---perhaps a bit of parmesan or
sour cream to drop on the top of each serving.

Polenta

Add 1 cup of polenta to 3-1/4 cup of warm
water along with a teaspoon of salt and 1
tablespoon of butter. Stir all ingredients until
mixed and then pour into a shallow pan and bake

at 350° for 50 to 60 minutes. Serve, warm with chicken and sauce.

CHICKEN PESTO SAUTE

2 boneless, skinless chicken breasts, sliced thinly
  on the diagonal
1 cup sliced mushrooms
1/2 cup sliced onion
1/2 cup sliced green or red pepper
1/2 to 1 cup any pesto
2 tablespoons butter or olive oil
8 to 12 ounces pasta, cooked and drained
1/2 cup shredded parmesan cheese

Slice chicken breasts thinly on the diagonal (it helps to freeze them slightly to slice), saute quickly in butter or oil <u>with</u> vegetables for about 2 minutes. Add cooked pasta and pesto and toss in the pan. Serve on a platter topped with parmesan cheese.

You can add additional vegetables if you wish. Or, substitute sea scallops for chicken. Yum!

BAKED CHICKEN PESTO

Insert 1/2 teaspoonsful of any of the green pestos under the skin in several places on a baking chicken. Rub the inside of the body cavity with pesto or mix pesto with stuffing. Bake at 350° until meat thermometer registers done. Brush chicken skin with pesto and leave in oven for another five minutes. Serve hot or cold, you may wish to serve plain pesto or pesto dressing as a condiment.

STUFFED CHICKEN BREASTS #1

NOTE: I generally use boneless breasts with skin intact, but the dishes will work well with skinless breasts.

4 chicken breasts
1 cup cooked wild or basmati rice
1 cup sliced mushrooms
1/2 cup chopped scallions or shallots
1/2 to 1 cup green pesto---I like Garlic
    Artichoke, Basil and Peppercorn

Flatten chicken breasts on underside only using the side of a heavy plate. Flatten between two sheets of waxed paper. Mix rice, mushrooms, scallions and pesto together. Use pesto to your taste. Place rice mixture on underside of chicken breast, roll breast and fasten with a toothpick, poultry pin or tie with kitchen string.

You can pan-brown breasts in butter and then bake at 350° until breasts are golden brown. You may pour a little white wine over them to bake if you like, and baste now and then.

STUFFED CHICKEN BREASTS #2

4 boneless chicken breasts
8 slices prosciutto
8 thin slices jack or swiss cheese
1/2 lb sliced mushrooms
1 bunch scallions, finely chopped
1/2 cup any green pesto
1 cup dry white wine
1/4 cup butter

Saute mushrooms and scallions in butter. Pound chicken breasts and arrange with skin side down to fill. Put two overlapping slices of prosciutto on each breast and top with each with 1/4 of the mushroom-onion mixture and 2 tablespoons of pesto. Top with overlapping slices of cheese and roll tightly securing with kitchen string in two places.

Place chicken seam side down in a shallow pan well greased with olive oil mist or other vegetable spray. Drizzle a teaspoon of melted butter over each breast and pour wine over all. Bake at 350° until golden brown, and do baste frequently. When done, clip and remove string, slice on the diagonal with a very sharp knife. Serve with pan juices.

More Stuffed Chicken Breasts

If you don't have time to fix your own, or your want some additional ideas for fillings, like crab and shrimp with jack cheese and pesto, spinach and ricotta with pesto, go to the Specialty Meats section at any upscale market and study the meat case. It boggles the mind and stimulates the imagination. I always go home with new ideas---and generally some meat for dinner.

PESTO-BASTED CHICKEN

1/2 cup pesto, cooks' choice
1/4 cup white wine
1/4 cup softened butter
Chicken pieces for four or four whole breasts

Mix pesto, wine and softened butter together and set aside while you prepare chicken for the oven or barbecue.

To bake: place chicken skin-side up in a shallow baking dish and brush with pesto mixture. Reserve some to use during baking process. Bake for 35 minutes at 350° and brush once or twice during the process with pesto mixture. Serve with pan juices.

To Barbecue: substitute melted butter and brush on breasts frequently while barbecuing. Heat remaining mixture and pour over chicken when serving.

STEVE'S AMBITIOUS POULTRY WITH PESTO STUFFING

If you are willing to bone a chicken or turkey (or if you can get someone to do it for you) this recipe is for you. If your significant other and you have the least spark of culinary ego madness, you can probably bait the trap and he/she will whisk the chore from your capable, but clever hands. Shuffle a bit, grumble, fake or provide a real-life demonstration of how inept you can be at the task. Manipulative, but ultimately rewarding to all parties---yes?

1 small turkey or large chicken
3 cups wild or basmati rice, cooked
1 cup sweet onion, sliced
1-1/2 cups sliced mushrooms
1/2 cup slivered almonds
1 cup thinly sliced water chestnuts
1 cup Garlic Artichoke, Basil, Peppercorn, or
    Tarragon pesto
1/2 cup melted butter
a little cooked pork sausage, if desired

Critical to the process is boning the bird, so do it first or con someone else into doing it while you make the dressing. This is not information I retain---I always need to look the process up in the Joy of Cooking.

Cook and drain sausage and mix with other ingredients. Mix thoroughly but with a light hand. Lay boned bird on work surface and place stuffing in a 2 inch wide line along the long side of the beast. Roll carefully and tightly and secure with poultry pins or string. You can also make more stuffing, fill the cavity and just wrap the bird around it once. Rub outside/skin with butter or vegetable shortening and place in 350° oven. Cook until golden brown, but always test the bird for doneness by inserting meat thermometer in the flesh in several places.

Note: I like to use poultry pins, even though they are a pain to clean after the fact. They don't leave bikini lines on the poultry like string---which is only important in presentation, but presentation is important, unless it's just you and the Cat.

Other chicken and turkey cuts/pieces do well marinated in pesto, olive oil and wine and broiled, baked or barbecued.

PESTO MARINADE

2 tablespoons pesto
1/4 cup oil
1/4 cup wine: white for green pestos, red wine
   for reds

Marinate for an hour or more then cook in your
favorite manner.

The chicken can also be sauted and when
finished a few tablespoons of heavy cream may
be added to the pan juices, simmered until
reduced and thickened and served with the
poultry or over rice or pasta.

This is the same marinade used for seafood.

Notes:

MEATS

Victoria's Bella Cucina

BEEF

Most people do not associate the taste of pesto with beef, but there are many applications, depending on your particular spice spectrum and preference. The Silverwater Cafe in Port Townsend is owned by David and Allison Hero. Allison, Celeste and Chris all use the pestos both for pastas and for seasoning. One of the dishes they did for visiting Goodwill dignitaries was a beef tenderloin stuffed with wild rice, mushrooms and Tarragon pesto.

If you are in Port Townsend, be certain to go there. They are open for lunch, have excellent food, a good wine selection, espresso and they serve the pestos from Victoria's. They were one of my first customers, they are one of my best customers and I love them dearly.

STEAKS

Rub with pesto of choice and barbecue or broil. Peppercorn, Garlic Artichoke, Tarragon and Basil.

Make a marinade of 2 tablespoons pesto, 1/4 cup olive oil and 1/2 cup of wine. Marinate steaks for 20 minutes then barbecue or broil.

Serve steak with Green Peppercorn or Garlic Artichoke pesto or pesto butter, drizzled on top.

Mix 1/4 cup of Sun-dried Tomato pesto per pound of ground beef and broil, fry in a non-stick pan, or barbecue.

BEEF ROASTS

I used to use lots of garlic and Basil, Garlic Artichoke or Green Peppercorn pesto with my beef roasts. My favorites are standing rib and cross rib roasts. I just cut slits in the roast and fill with pesto, or rub the roast with pesto before putting it in the oven. Instead of horseradish sauce, I serve Green Peppercorn or Garlic Artichoke pesto either plain or mixed half and half with sour cream.

I love pot roast done the old-fashioned way in the oven, or in the electric skillet or oven with vegetables. To season with pesto, rub roast before pan browning and add 1/4 cup of pesto to the pan liquid, basting the veggies when you add them. This is for the green pestos. Try the combination of Sun-dried Tomato pesto to a combination of beef bouillon and red wine---2 parts bouillon/broth to 1 part wine.

For more Sun-dried Tomato pesto, I brown the pot roast in an electric skillet with a sliced onion and a cup or two of sliced mushrooms. Then add 1 cup of red pesto and 1-1/2 cups of red wine and cook until tender. This can also be done in an oven or a crock pot, and you can add whatever vegetable desired during the last 20 minutes of cooking time.

BEEF SUN-DRIED TOMATO

2 to 3 pounds bottom round, fat trimmed
2 tablespoons olive oil
1 tablespoon butter
1/2 cup chopped onion
1/2 cup Sun-dried Tomato pesto
2 cloves garlic, chopped or pressed
1 cup tomato purée
1/2 cup beef stock---I use bouillon from the
    natural foods section---no MSG please

Brown meat in olive oil. Transfer to dutch oven or suitable substitute. Saute onions and garlic in butter until tender. Mix in pesto and place on top of meat. Mix beef stock and tomato purée and pour over the top. Cover and bake for 3 hours at 350°.

This dish can also be done in a crockpot---low all day or high for half day.

MEATLOAF

There are a few tricks to meatloaf.

1. Your grandmother may swear by it, but under no circumstances ever put oatmeal in meatloaf.

2. Never put dry bread crumbs in your meatloaf. In fact, don't use commercial bread crumbs. Take a piece of sourdough or wheat bread and tear it into small chunks. Place the bread chunks (1/2 inch square or so) in a bowl and cover with milk or red wine. Put the whole soppy lot in your meatloaf.

3. You don't really need veal for meatloaf---it's expensive and its delicate flavor can get lost. Use lean ground beef and a good quality country pork sausage. One pound pork to three pounds lean beef is my formula.

4. Use lots of **real** garlic, and/or 1/2 cup of pesto.

5. Add 1 or 2 eggs to hold it together.

6. Don't let anyone or any cookbook suggest rolling anything, no matter how tasty, jelly roll style inside a meatloaf. This is an absolutely impossible task.

7. Pour a cup of boiling water over the meatloaf before you put it in the oven.

VICTORIA'S MEATLOAF

1 pound good quality country pork sausage
3 pounds lean ground beef
3 to 6 strips lean, nitrate-free bacon
1 cup diced onion
1/2 cup any green or red pesto
more garlic if desired---2 cloves shot through
    the press suggested
2 eggs
1 slice sourdough bread torn into small chunks
    and soaked in milk or red wine

Put bread in milk or wine to soak. Place all other ingredients except bacon in a large bowl, add bread and milk and mix thoroughly with your hands---there is really no other way to do this except in the food processor and doing by hand gives you a better product and less to wash. Shape meat mixture into a loaf, place in roasting pan, put bacon strips on top and pour 1 cup boiling water over loaf. Bake at 350° until thermometer registers 170° in the center of the loaf.

STUFFED PEPPERS

I use the meatloaf recipe to do my stuffed
peppers, using 1/2 of everything to do 6 to 8
peppers. I like to cut the peppers in half,
allowing more meat and less pepper. Heap
pepper halves with meat mixture, place meat side
up in shallow baking dish and bake for 35-40
minutes at 350°.

MEATBALLS WITH PESTO

Use the same recipe for meatloaf, shape into
meatballs, brown and add to your sauce.

VEAL

VEAL MAISON WITH PESTO

1-1/2 lb veal shoulder, bone in or boneless
1/4 cup olive oil
1 onion, medium, chopped finely
1 cup sliced fresh mushrooms
1 cup tomato juice (yes, here it is again)
1/2 cup white wine
2 tablespoons Basil or Peppercorn pesto

Bone meat and remove fat. Cut into thin strips
about 1 inch wide and 2 inches long. Saute
meat in oil, lightly browning it. Add the sliced
onions and mushrooms, cooking until golden.

Add wine, tomato juice, pesto and a bit of cracked or fresh ground black pepper. Cover and simmer for 25 minutes. Serve in bowls with crusty bread and a salad.

STUFFED BREAST OF VEAL

1 breast of veal with pocket

Stuffing
2 cups bread cubes or rice for stuffing
mushrooms
water chestnuts
chopped walnuts
1/2 cup butter
1/2 cup Garlic Artichoke or Peppercorn pesto
Extra pesto to rub on veal

Mix ingredients for stuffing and fill pocket, securing with poultry pins. Rub the breast with pesto and sear it on both sides until nicely browned. Add the wine and cook in a 325° oven 20 minutes per pound. Either cook in a covered roaster or cover with foil. Place extra stuffing in a small covered bowl and bake with veal.

When the veal is done, make a sauce using the pan juices. For sauce, melt 3 tablespoons of butter and saute one onion. Then add 3 tablespoons of flour, 1 cup of white wine or 1 cup broth, pan juices minus excess fat and stir until thickened. Stir in cream and a tablespoon more of pesto---simmer a few minutes and then serve with breast slices.

VEAL CUTLETS OR SCALLOPS

Saute veal cutlets or scallops and sliced mushrooms in butter, then add pesto and a 1/2 cup of white wine. When liquid is slightly reduced add a little heavy cream and serve veal with mushrooms sauce.

VEAL PARMIGIANA PESTO

This dish uses Sun-dried Tomato pesto to flavor the tomato sauce---actually to kick it into overdrive.

4 to 6 boneless veal cutlets
1 cup Sun-dried Tomato pesto
1 cup tomato sauce (canned)
1 tablespoon olive oil
1 tablespoon butter
1/2 cup Basil pesto
12 ounces mozzarella cheese, cut into 4 or 6
    slices
3/4 cup parmesan cheese
breadcrumbs

Mix parmesan and breadcrumbs in a shallow dish and pre-heat broiler. Mix tomato sauce and Sun-Dried Tomato pesto. Flatten veal between two pieces of waxed paper until thin. Coat the veal in the parmesan and breadcrumbs. Heat the oil and butter in a skillet and saute veal for 2 minutes per side, then place the veal in a shallow oven-proof dish. Cover/top each piece of veal with 1/3 to 1/2 cup of the tomato sauce, mixed with Sun-dried Tomato pesto. Lay the cheese slices on top and broil until cheese is bubbly, garnish each slice with 1 tablespoon of basil pesto and serve.

You can play around with the cheese in this dish ---provolone, buffalo mozzarella, jack or brie. The choice is yours.

LAMB

RACK OF LAMB POUR DEUX

1 rack of lamb cut into two equal portions
1/2 cup Garlic Artichoke or Green Peppercorn
2 tablespoons cornmeal
2 tablespoons olive oil

Set oven at 400°. Brush olive oil lightly on lamb. Combine cornmeal and pesto and coat the lamb. Place in a shallow roasting pan and roast to desired doneness using meat thermometer to test. 25 minutes should yield medium rare results. Slice and serve.

LEG OF LAMB

6 to 8 lb leg of lamb
3 cloves garlic, peeled and slivered
1/2 to 1 cup Garlic Artichoke or Peppercorn
    pesto
1/4 cup olive oil
salt to taste may be added to pesto, if desired
quartered new potatoes

Insert the slivered garlic into slits cut in the leg
of lamb with a sharp knife. (I emphasize sharp
because in Nana's kitchen you could ride to
Boston on any of her knives. Any time relatives
came over for dinner they started to sharpen her
knives---magically, they were dull in a day. She
also had some quirky ability to stop watches
within a day of strapping them on her wrist).
Anyway, add the olive oil to the pesto and coat
the lamb completely. Place in a shallow roasting
pan. Place the potatoes in a bowl with the left
over pesto and a little bit more olive oil and coat
potatoes with mixture and arrange around the
lamb. Cook at 425° for 45 minutes then reduce
heat to 375° and cook for 30 minutes or when
registers done on meat thermometer. Move
potatoes around now and then with a slotted
spoon to keep them from sticking.

Remove roast and potatoes to a serving platter
and garnish with fresh parsley or more pesto.

BONELESS LEG OF LAMB WITH PESTO STUFFING

5 to 6 lb butterflied leg of lamb
1 cup mushrooms
1 package frozen spinach, thawed or one bunch fresh spinach, washed and chopped
1 bunch scallions, finely chopped
8 ounces boursin
1 cup Garlic Artichoke or Peppercorn pesto

Pre-heat oven to 425°. Saute mushrooms lightly in 1 tablespoon butter and 1 tablespoon oil. In a bowl combine spinach, scallions, boursin and 1/2 cup pesto, thinned with a little olive oil (crumble boursin with a fork before adding). When mixture is prepared, lay out the lamb on a large work surface and spread the spinach mixture evenly overall. Then roll the lamb into a "jelly roll" and tie with kitchen string. Coat the roast with remaining pesto and bake to personal taste, using meat thermometer placed in the thickest part to gauge doneness. Cut into 1/2 inch slices---serve hot or cold.

These slices make great next-day sandwiches or take-along food, served with a little extra pesto as a condiment.

STUFFED LAMBCHOPS

With the availability of lamb improving in the
marketplace, custom cuts are more frequently
found at the meat counter. If you like lamb,
thick chops are excellent with a pesto stuffing,
and done on the barbecue. Put pesto in the slit
cut for stuffing or use your favorite stuffing
mixture laced with pesto. Brush the outside with
pesto and bake, barbecue or broil. I like Garlic
Artichoke, but the Basil and Peppercorn are also
good.

Serve with a bit of pesto or light pesto cream
sauce on top.

Pesto cream sauce: melt 2 tablespoons of
butter, add 2 tablespoons of flour and a cup of
cold milk. Keep stirring until thickened, add 1/4
to 1/2 cup of pesto and serve.

PORK

I have a friend who refuses to eat pork. His
reasoning is that pigs do not sweat. He was in
FFA so he should know, but who knows, he
could be telling a pigtale. Regardless, I love
pork and so does my Cat, Finnegan. And,....
pork loves pesto.

BARBECUED PORK CHOPS

4 to 6 pork chops (1 inch thick), rib, loin or best
    of all, center cut
2 tablespoons pesto (green)
1 tablespoon olive oil
1 tablespoon white wine---optional

Mix pesto, oil and wine together. Place pork
chops in a shallow dish or pan and pour
marinade over the top. In 30 minutes turn and
marinate for another 30 minutes. Barbecue or
broil and serve with extra pesto as a condiment.
I generally use the Peppercorn, Basil or Garlic
Artichoke and just place a small dollop---say a
teaspoon---on top of each chop before serving.

Note: The emergency gourmet can simply dip
each pork chop in the mixture and place on the
barbecue, basting a couple of times during the
process.

STUFFED PORK CHOPS

Stuff pork chops with pure pesto or your favorite
stuffing flavored with pesto. I like to mix 1/4 to
1/2 cup pesto with chopped walnuts and some
jack or brie cheese. Amounts of all ingredients
vary according to number of chops. For two
chops I use 1/4 cup pesto, 2 tablespoons coarsely
chopped walnuts and 1/2 cup cheese, shredded or
cubed.

Brush outside with pesto and barbecue, bake or broil.

Stuffed Pork Chops can be served topped with a bit of pesto or pesto cream sauce.

PORK CHOPS IN SOUR CREAM

6 loin pork chops---1/2 inch thick
1/2 cup + 1 tablespoon Garlic Artichoke or
    Peppercorn pesto
2 tablespoon olive oil
2 medium onions sliced
1/2 cup white wine
1 cup sour cream
salt and pepper to taste

Rub chops with 1 tablespoon of pesto and brown lightly on both sides in olive oil. Remove excess fat and add sliced onions. Add wine, cover and simmer for 25 minutes. When done, remove meat to platter and add sour cream and remaining pesto, mixed together, to the pan. Cook until the mixture just boils then serve over pork chops and garnish with chopped parsley.

SCALLOPED POTATOES
AND PORK CHOPS

Nana always made her scalloped potatoes with
ham from a neighboring farmer's smokehouse. I
prefer pork chops because they are less of a
threat on the sodium spectrum and don't contain
any nitrates, although as we all now know,
thanks to John Luchow, former Future Farmer,
pigs don't sweat. If anyone knows the
significance of this please, let me know---even
you, John. Meanwhile, the Cat and I continue to
eat pork now and then.

Lightly brown 4 to 6 rib or loin pork chops in a
tablespoon of oil, in a non-stick pan. Drain on
paper towels.

Prepare 1 recipe for SCALLOPED POTATOES
PESTO from the vegetable section of this book.
(I lied---you need to refer back for this one.)
Place browned pork chops on the final layer of
potatoes and cover with milk/cream mixed with
pesto and a 1/2 cup white wine. Bake for 50
minutes at 350°, and again, I think a little cheese
on top in the final stages can't hurt. Remember
to drizzle with pesto just before placing on the
table---or after you put it on the table---or just
after you take it out of the oven. I refuse to get
obsessed with order and portion size, which is
exactly why I can't make a souffle or an
angelfood cake.

I am certain that pesto would be wonderful in a salmon or cheese souffle, but someone else is going to need to be responsible for development of those recipes. I don't even want to accept the liability for trying.

ROAST PORK WITH PESTO

There are a number of options here. I generally coat a pork loin roast or pork tenderloin with Peppercorn or Garlic Artichoke pesto and slow roast at 350°. In the case of the tenderloin, barbecue on a gas grill. I first make little slits in the roast into which I place either garlic slivers or pesto, then slather the outside with pesto and baste midway through the process.

If you are lucky enough to find a boneless, rolled pork roast---or you have a butcher whose meat is all as tender as his heart, (this being the axiom of Bill Benedetto the famous former butcher, to the Aldrich Brothers Store in Port Townsend) ---you can do a stuffed pork roast with a bread, rice, or vegetable stuffing flavored with pesto. I think it might also be tasty to simply spread the inside of the roast with the Sun-dried Tomato then re-roll and roast---slice thinly and serve with pan juices. To stuff---cut the strings on the roast and spread completely with stuffing of choice. Dot a teaspoon of pesto here and there and then roll tightly in jelly roll style and secure with kitchen string. In some spots, kitchen string is *de rigueur.*

Cooking time will vary with the sizing of the roast and I always suggest the use of a meat thermometer with pork, having been terrorized with pork horror stories by a series of Italian butchers who worked for my father. With a rolled, stuffed roast, make certain that the meat thermometer is in the center and in the meat--- not the stuffing. Since the meat is denser, you will feel the resistance when you hit it. Internal temperature should register 165 to 170°.

ROAST PORK WITH WINE AND PESTO

4 to 5 pound pork roast
1/3 cup butter
1 chopped onion
6 whole cloves
1/2 cup Peppercorn pesto
3/4 cup dry white wine

Brown meat in butter on all sides in a Dutch oven. Add onion, mix wine with pesto and add. Cover and simmer over low heat for 2 hours. Strain the sauce and serve with pork.

PORK CROWN ROAST

At Christmas time, 1990, I saw an absolutely beautiful crown roast in the Chef Cuts Section of the Totem Lake Larry's, only to see it being rerouted to the Bellevue Larry's under the careful guidance of Michael. Snooze and lose, but the beauty of Larry's is that they can usually fix you up with the roast's brother if you ask nicely and smile.

4 to 5 lb crown roast of pork (tied at crown and loin)
1/2 cup Garlic Artichoke, Peppercorn or Basil Pesto
2 tablespoons olive oil
1/2 cup white wine

Place roast in a shallow roasting pan with the bone ends down. Insert meat thermometer in loin part of roast, not in fat and not touching bone. Roast at 325°, until meat thermometer registers 165 to 170°. After placing roast in oven, mix other ingredients together and baste the roast with mixture four times during the last hour of roasting.

Notes:

One 4 lb package boneless, skinless chicken
   breasts
1 package frozen shrimp or scallops
2 or 3 packages frozen fresh pasta
1 to 2 lb dry pasta---linguine and raditore
   preferred
2 loaves crusty bread, wrapped and frozen
2 Boboli crusts-wrapped and frozen
frozen focaccia
2 jars quality red pasta sauce
1 lb shredded parmesan, frozen
1 lb shredded mozzarella, frozen
8 ounces cream cheese-lasts forever if wrapped
   properly
6 to 8 ounces brie, frozen
black olives
1 can or jar artichoke hearts
Tuscany Toast
2 pints Vanilla Hagen-Daz
Amaretto for the Hagen-Daz
Dry white wine
Red table wine
1 package frozen vegetables suitable for pasta
1 lb butter, frozen
Several 8 ounce tubs of *PESTO PESTO*-at least
   one Garlic Artichoke, one green, and the
   Sun-dried Tomato
PESTO PESTO COOKBOOK

With the foregoing ingredients you are set for
drop-ins and emergencies. Actually frozen pesto,
dry pasta, some parmesan and bread should do it,
but if you want to achieve a state of complete

readiness keep the above list in mind. Rotate and serve to family members as time dictates. Replace as needed.

Notes:

INDEX

Notes:

TO ORDER BY MAIL

PESTO PESTO Cookbooks make excellent gifts for friends, as will our pestos. Pesto keeps well in the refrigerator for two months, and freezes beautifully for up to a year.

By mail, Pesto Paks are available as follows:
TRY PAK: Three 8 oz. tubs of Pesto Pesto, $15.95 plus $3.00 shipping & handling, each ($18.95)

CASE PAK: Twelve 8 oz. tubs of Pesto Pesto, $62.00 plus $5.00 shipping & handling per pak ($67.00)

PLEASE SEND ME:

☐ ____ *PESTO PESTO* Cookbooks @ $10.95 ($13.00 Canadian) plus $1.00 each S & H

☐ **TRY PAK #1**
Basil
Sun-Dried Tomato
Garlic Artichoke

☐ **TRY PAK #2**
All one flavor
Specify Flavor:
_____

CASE PAKS:

☐ 4 Basil
4 Sun-Dried Tomato
4 Garlic Artichoke

☐ All one flavor
Specify flavor:
_____

Wholesale inquiries invited. Washington residents, please add 7.8% sales tax. Please send check or money order to: PESTO PESTO • Victoria's Bella Cucina • P.O. Box 1011 • Olalla, WA 98359

Check or M.O. enclosed for the amt. of _____

Name _____

Address _____

City/State/ZIP _____   Phone _____

TO ORDER BY MAIL

PESTO PESTO Cookbooks make excellent gifts for friends, as will our pestos. Pesto keeps well in the refrigerator for two months, and freezes beautifully for up to a year.

By mail, Pesto Paks are available as follows:
TRY PAK: Three 8 oz. tubs of Pesto Pesto,
$15.95 plus $3.00 shipping & handling, each ($18.95)

CASE PAK: Twelve 8 oz. tubs of Pesto Pesto,
$62.00 plus $5.00 shipping & handling per pak ($67.00)

PLEASE SEND ME:

☐ ____ *PESTO PESTO* Cookbooks @ $10.95
($13.00 Canadian) plus $1.00 each S & H

☐ **TRY PAK #1**   ☐ **TRY PAK #2**
Basil   All one flavor
Sun-Dried Tomato   Specify Flavor:
Garlic Artichoke   _____

CASE PAKS:

☐ 4 Basil   ☐ All one flavor
4 Sun-Dried Tomato   Specify flavor:
4 Garlic Artichoke   _____

Wholesale inquiries invited. Washington residents, please add 7.8% sales tax. Please send check or money order to: PESTO PESTO • Victoria's Bella Cucina • P.O. Box 1011 • Olalla, WA 98359

Check or M.O. enclosed for the amt. of _____

Name _____

Address _____

City/State/ZIP_____ Phone _____